A Traveler's Companion to North Dakota State Historic Sites

2nd Edition

Edited by
J. Signe Snortland

STATE HISTORICAL SOCIETY OF NORTH DAKOTA

State Historical Society of North Dakota
Merlan E. Paaverud, Director
North Dakota Heritage Center, Bismarck, ND 58505
1996, 2002

CONTRIBUTING AUTHORS:
Walter L. Bailey, Merl Paaverud, J. Signe Snortland,
Fern E. Swenson, and Ronald Warner

PUBLICATIONS EDITOR (1st Edition):
Janet Daley

PUBLICATIONS EDITOR (2nd Edition):
Kathleen Davison

A traveler's companion to North Dakota state historic sites / edited by J. Signe
    Snortland.—Bismarck, ND : State Historical Society of North Dakota, 1996, 2002.
    xii, 164 p.: ill., maps (1 folded), plans, ports.; 24 cm.
    Credits: Contributing authors, Walter L. Bailey, Merl Paaverud, J. Signe Snortland,
Fern E. Swenson, and Ronald Warner; publications editors, Janet Daley, Kathleen
Davison.
    Partial funding by the North Dakota Humanities Council.
    Includes "Endnotes" and index.
    1. Historic sites—North Dakota—Guidebooks. 2. North Dakota—Description and
Travel. 3. North Dakota—History. I. Snortland, J. Signe. II. State Historical Society of
North Dakota. III. North Dakota Humanities Council.

I.P. / 2M / 02

Contents

Lakes and Gardens

The Valley

Denotes sites or museums that are not administered by the State Historical Society of North Dakota.

Preface

This book is the result of an extraordinary team effort by the staff of the State Historical Society of North Dakota. We owe no small debt of gratitude to the book's editor, J. Signe Snortland, the former chief archeologist for the Society, who not only contributed the narrative on many of the sites described within the book but also coordinated the research and writing by the contributing authors, a challenging task in a collaborative effort like this one. We also appreciate and acknowledge the work of the other contributing authors: Walter L. Bailey, planner in the Historic Preservation Division; Merl Paaverud, then director of the Historic Sites Division; Fern E. Swenson, then chief archeologist in the Historic Preservation Division; and Ronald Warner, administrative officer, all at the State Historical Society of North Dakota. Brian R. Austin, graphic designer in the Museum and Education Division, photographed many of the sites, created the graphics and the maps, and designed the layout of the book.

As always, our gratitude is extended to Everett Albers and the North Dakota Humanities Council, an affiliate of the National Endowment for the Humanities, for their financial support. Thanks are also due to those who read and commented on this manuscript while it was taking shape: Mary Jane Schneider, J. Michael McCormack, Fred Schneider, Gerard Baker, Dorreen Yellow Bird, Frank Vyzralek, Tom Shay, Patricia Jessen, and many of the staff of the State Historical Society of North Dakota. Their comments and suggestions were invaluable and much appreciated.

This guidebook is designed to help you find the sites that will awaken your interest in North Dakota's lively and varied past. Unlike in more populated states, North Dakota's state historic site network offers limitless and unique opportunities to view locations where western history unfolded in the original context of untouched, rural landscapes. The "Introduction to North Dakota's Past," which follows on page ix, gives a brief overview of the state's history and explains where and how each historic site contributed to that history from the time of its first human inhabitants through the late nineteenth century, a span of almost 12,000 years. Because many of the sites relate directly to the military activities of General Henry H. Sibley and General Alfred Sully and their troops during their 1863 expeditions to Dakota Territory, a brief history of that military operation is provided on page 61.

The following map divides the state into four geographic regions. The state historic sites are listed alphabetically within each geographic region. Each site is marked by a symbol that indicates its significance in one of five areas of the state's history: Aboriginal Americans, Exploration and Settlement, Trade and Technology, State Government, and Military Affairs. The sites are indexed alphabetically and also by these thematic areas on page 163. In the main part of the book, the contributing authors have written a brief description and history of each site, with illustrations and maps showing the location of each accessible site. In the last section of the book, we have listed other historic sites, state and federal parks, and historic museums to visit within a fifty-mile radius of each site.

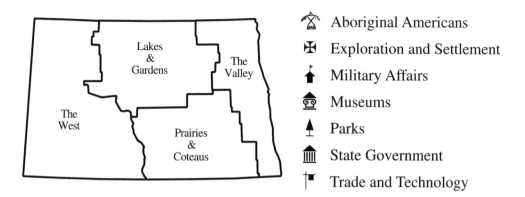

Although this book focuses on the fifty-six state historic sites and markers adminis-tered by the Society, there are many other intriguing and exciting places to visit for those interested in history of the northern plains. North Dakotans and visitors will enjoy a trip to the North Dakota Heritage Center on the capitol grounds in Bismarck, home to the State Historical Society of North Dakota. There, permanent museum ex-hibits tell the broad story of North Dakota's past and also offer many temporary exhib-its, highlighting specific people, places, events, or artifacts that bring the state's history to life for visitors from all over the globe. For your research or questions about North Dakota history, you may wish to visit the State Archives and Historical Research Li-brary in the Heritage Center as well. In the northeastern corner of the state, the Society's Pembina State Museum brings to light the agricultural history of the Red River Valley and the importance of the region in early trade networks, the lifeways of the Chippewa and Métis peoples who were among the area's earliest inhabitants, and the settlement of Euro-American immigrants.

This second edition also includes information about an additional six sites and/or museums that are part of the National Park Service, state park system, or are privately run but which relate to significant part of the state's history and offer visitors a look at some of North Dakota's most beautiful landscapes and important natural history fea-tures. In the western region, those sites are Fort Abraham Lincoln State Park, Fort Union Trading Post National Historic Site, Knife River Indian Villages National His-toric Site, and Theodore Roosevelt National Park. In the lakes and gardens region, they are Fort Mandan and the North Dakota Lewis and Clark Interpretive Center at Washburn.

North Dakota is also the home to hundreds of properties listed on the State Historic Sites Registry and the National Register of Historic Places, which are official lists of buildings, structures, districts, sites, objects, and traditional cultural properties signifi-cant in local or national history. More information on those historic properties is avail-able by contacting the Historic Preservation Division, State Historical Society of North

Dakota, 612 East Boulevard Avenue, Bismarck, North Dakota, 58505, or by calling (701) 328-2666.

You can help preserve North Dakota's history with a membership in the State Historical Society of North Dakota Foundation. The foundation's mission is to increase awareness about, participation in, and development of North Dakota's historic legacies through financial support of the work of the State Historical Society of North Dakota. Membership allows you free admission to all North Dakota state historic sites, and all members receive *North Dakota History*, a quarterly journal, and *Plains Talk*, the Society's quarterly newsletter. For more information about membership and additional benefits, please contact the State Historical Society of North Dakota Foundation, Box 1976, Bismarck, North Dakota 58502-1976, or call (701) 222-1966.

We hope that as you tour our great state you will come to appreciate the wonderful legacy that our state's historic sites offer to this generation of visitors and all those to come.

Janet Daley and Kathleen Davison
Publications Editors
1996, 2002

Editor's Note: Much of the information about the events and conditions at the state historic sites related to the Sibley and Sully expeditions of 1863 came from extensive research in the holdings of the State Archives and Historical Research Library. The holdings include a few original diaries and transcripts of several others. Some of these diaries are anonymous, while others were written by the soldiers, surgeons, and, in one case, by a civilian who was hired as a teamster. (Please see the endnotes on page 146 for specific citations.) These narratives tell of the difficult challenges the men on these expeditions faced. Military reports and records and other documents in the archives, as well as some published books, were consulted. While more Indian accounts of this period of conflict on the northern plains have been published in recent years, there are, unfortunately, fewer primary sources of the Indian perspective available for researchers.

The Dakota (Sioux) are made up of four Santee divisions, the two Yankton and Yanktonai divisions, and the Lakota (Teton) division. Each of these divisions are divided into groups, closely allied but made up of individual bands or camps. In this book, we have used the specific names of Indian bands when they could be verified but used the name Dakota or Sioux when more specific data was unavailable.

Foreword

Welcome to North Dakota's state historic sites. An upsurge in heritage tourism across the country has created a renewed interest in the history of the northern plains. North Dakota is fortunate to be the home of many significant historic sites. A visit to any of the historic sites and museums described in this guidebook will allow you to experience firsthand the places where some of our state's pivotal historic events transpired. Stand in an earthlodge depression at Double Ditch and imagine the sounds of the busy Mandan Indian village that once existed there. Travel to Fort Buford, a Dakota Territory military compound near the Montana border, and visualize the soldiers' survival during a hard winter on the northern plains frontier. Visit Gingras, near Walhalla, and experience a Métis fur trader's log home and trading post set in the Pembina Hills.

This book will serve as a helpful guide as you visit any or all of these exciting locations. Some sites are well developed with interpreters, visitors' centers with exhibits, furnished buildings, picnic areas, and other amenities (see page 147 for checklist of facilities). Others lie obscurely in pastures without a monument or fencepost to mark their existence. A few of the sites are currently closed to visitors because of lack of accessibility, concerns about preservation, or out of respect for American Indians who hold some of these places sacred.

We invite you to enjoy North Dakota's heritage but ask that you remember to take nothing but photographs. The past belongs to everyone, and all artifacts must be left behind for the information they represent and for future visitors to enjoy. It is illegal to search for or to remove artifacts from state, federal, or tribal property without a permit.

For further information about any of the State Historical Society's sites, write to the State Historical Society of North Dakota, 612 East Boulevard Avenue, Bismarck, North Dakota, 58505, call (701) 328-2666, or check our web site at www.DiscoverND.com/hist.

Merl Paaverud
Director
State Historical Society of North Dakota

Introduction to North Dakota's Past

North Dakota's history began thousands of years ago when glaciers covered much of the northern hemisphere, including part of what is now North Dakota. The state's human heritage began with the first people who lived here. Most scientists believe the first inhabitants of North America entered the New World during glacial times, when Asia and North America were connected, by crossing this land bridge. Descendants of these first people, American Indians, have passed down oral histories that speak of their people originating in the New World.

The earliest artifacts found in this state were made by these first people, called Paleo-Indians, who hunted mammoth, very large bison, and other now-extinct large mammals. The Paleo-Indian period dates from 9500 to 5500 B.C. At **Crowley Flint Quarry**, deep pits dug by people seeking Knife River flint, a prized rock used for making stone tools, testify to the industriousness of these early inhabitants.

As the Ice Age ended, the glaciers retreated to the north, and the climate became hotter and drier. Grasslands replaced the vast boreal forest that covered the area that would become North Dakota. People adapted to the change in environment by hunting smaller game animals and gathering prairie plants during the Archaic period, dating from 5500 B.C. to 400 B.C. Artifacts that appear to date from this time period were discovered buried at the **Camp Hancock** site.

As the climate moderated and became similar to the modern environment, trade brought northern people into contact with other tribes living to the east along the Ohio and Illinois Rivers. In addition to trade goods, new ideas traveled along these exchange routes. The concept of interring deceased relatives, together with exotic trade items, in artificial earthen hills called burial mounds, spread westward. From 400 B.C. until A.D. 1000, during the Woodland period, mounds were used to bury the dead. The **Pulver Mounds** and **Standing Rock** sites preserve Woodland period burial mounds.

The introduction of imported domesticated plants, such as maize, squash, pumpkins, sunflowers, and beans, transformed some of the nomadic Woodland people into village-dwelling people. During the Plains Village period (A.D. 1000 to 1780) the Mandan, Hidatsa, Arikara, and Cheyenne lived in villages along the Missouri River and other major rivers. The early Mandan and Hidatsa villagers built rectangular houses near their river-bottom gardens between A.D. 1100 and 1600. **Menoken Indian Village**, **Huff Indian Village**, and the **Fort Mandan Overlook** sites were occupied by these early farmers.

By the end of the sixteenth century, the rectangular earthlodge was replaced by a smaller, circular earthen house. **Double Ditch Indian Village**, **Molander Indian Vil-**

lage, the **Knife River Indian Villages**, On-A-Slant Indian Village at **Fort Abraham Lincoln State Park**, and the village at the **Fort Clark** site are Mandan, Hidatsa, and Arikara earthlodge villages, occupied between A.D. 1600 and 1861.

Although the dates of their creation are unknown, American Indian rock art sites are found at **Medicine Rock**, **Writing Rock**, and **Turtle Effigy** sites. These rare places preserve such important symbols as the outline of a turtle in boulders and numerous other animal figures carved into rocks.

The first European explorers entered this area in the 1700s. The earliest recorded European visit was a 1738 expedition headed by Pierre Gaultier de Varennes, the Sieur de la Vérendrye, a French fur trader. He and his sons departed from a fort in the area that would become the city of Winnipeg, Manitoba, and stayed at a Mandan earthlodge village (see **Menoken Indian Village**). The location of the village that hosted la Vérendrye and his sons is still a matter of debate.

In 1797 David Thompson mapped the Northwest Company's fur posts from the Souris River to the western shore of Lake Superior. The **David Thompson** site commemo-

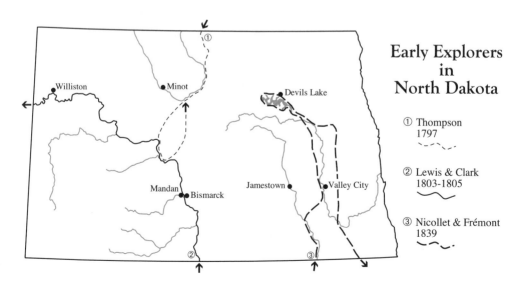

Early Explorers in North Dakota

Williston • • Minot Devils Lake

Mandan • Bismarck Jamestown • • Valley City

① Thompson 1797

② Lewis & Clark 1803-1805

③ Nicollet & Frémont 1839

rates his visit to North Dakota. The Lewis and Clark expedition, led by Captains Meriwether Lewis and William Clark, was the first governmental exploration of the Louisiana Purchase. This journey up the Mississippi and Missouri rivers to the Pacific Ocean began in May 1804 and ended in September 1806. During the winter of 1804/1805, the expedition stayed in a winter encampment called Fort Mandan, near the villages of the Mandan and Hidatsa Indians at the mouth of the Knife River. Upon their return from the Pacific Ocean, they stopped to visit these villages again in August 1806. **Knife River Indian Villages National Historic Site** preserves the site of several of these villages. A reproduction of **Fort Mandan** has been constructed along the Missouri River close to Washburn, North Dakota. Nearby is the **North Dakota Lewis and Clark Interpretive Center** which houses displays that focus on the time the expedition spent at Fort Mandan and on the fur trader era that followed. Other early explorers, Joseph Nicollet and John C. Frémont, investigated the area between the Mississippi and Missouri rivers in 1839. The **Lake Jessie** site is one of their camps.

Explorers were quickly followed by fur traders. **Fort Clark** contains the remains of two early-nineteenth-century fur trade posts (Fort Clark Trading Post and Primeau's Post) that were established to trade with nearby Mandan and, later, Arikara people. **Fort Union**, established near the confluence of the Yellowstone and Missouri Rivers, was one of the most significant fur-trading posts ever erected. **Gingras Trading Post** preserves the original 1840s home and trading post of Métis businessman and legislator Antoine Blanc Gingras. Norman Kittson's fur trade warehouse from the 1840s at **Walhalla** is a preserved remnant of the commercial enterprise of the American Fur Company.

By the mid-nineteenth century, settlers were replacing the fur traders, and the military came to protect this Euro-American migration to the West. **Fort Abercrombie**, built in 1858, is the oldest military post in the state. In 1863 General Henry H. Sibley led an army across Dakota Territory, pursuing a group of Dakota who were believed to have participated in the Dakota Conflict of 1862 (see **Sibley and Sully Expeditions of 1863**). State historic sites from this expedition are **Buffalo Creek**, **Big Mound Battlefield**, **Chaska (Camp Banks)**, **Lake Johnson**, **McPhail's Butte Overlook**, **Camp Arnold**, **Camp Atchison**, **Camp Buell**, **Camp Corning**, **Camp Grant**, **Camp Kimball**, **Camp Sheardown**, **Camp Weiser**, and **Camp Whitney**.

General Alfred Sully and the 2,000 soldiers in his command were also part of the military reprisal following the Dakota Conflict of 1862. **Whitestone Hill Battlefield** marks the site of the 1863 battle, which was the bloodiest engagement fought in North Dakota. **Fort Rice**, established in 1864, served as a base for Sully's 1864 and 1865 expeditions. As part of his 1864 expedition, Sully reluctantly escorted a wagon train bound for the Montana gold fields. **Sully's Heart River Corral** preserves rifle pits dug by frightened gold seekers left behind when the general attacked a Dakota Indian encampment at **Killdeer Mountain Battlefield**. Another wagon train of immigrants led by Captain James L. Fisk, on its way from Fort Rice in 1864, was attacked by Hunkpapa Sioux who were angered by the military reprisals of Sibley and Sully. At a location now named **Fort Dilts**, the immigrants drew their wagons in a circle, built a sod wall around them, and waited to be rescued by the army.

Fort Ransom, established on the Sheyenne River in 1867, and **Fort Totten**, constructed near Devils Lake between 1867 and 1873, provided protection for settlers headed for western gold fields. At **Fort Totten** sixteen original structures still stand, and both the military mission of the post and its later use as an Indian boarding school are interpreted at the site. In 1872 an infantry post, originally named Fort McKeen, was established on a Missouri River bluff to protect railroad surveyors and work crews. A year later a cavalry post was constructed on the river bottoms below Fort McKeen and both installations were renamed **Fort Abraham Lincoln**. In 1876, the fort's first commander, Lt. Col. George Armstrong Custer, and the Seventh Cavalry rode out on their ill-fated campaign that ended at the Battle of the Little Bighorn.

Troops from **Camp Hancock** guarded workers building the Northern Pacific Railroad at Bismarck. Camp Hancock later became a supply distribution point for forts further out on the frontier. **Fort Buford**, the sentinel of the north from 1866 until 1895, was one of the forts protecting river transportation. The fort is also the place where the Hunkpapa Sioux leader Sitting Bull surrendered. The **Sitting Bull Burial** site near Fort Yates is a memorial to this Indian leader.

Palmer's Spring, **Bismarck-Deadwood Stage Trail**, **Cannonball Stage Station**, **Steamboat Warehouse**, **Maple Creek Crossing**, and **Brenner Crossing** mark sites associated with transportation, including historic overland travel, steamboats, and river crossings.

As the Indian Wars drew to a close, settlers began to move into the state in greater numbers. **Hudson Townsite**, **St. Claude**, **Sweden**, and **Wadeson Cabin** commemorate late-nineteenth-century settlements and related activities. **Oak Lawn Church** marks the cemetery and foundation of an 1885 Presbyterian church. One of the oldest churches in Bismarck now stands at **Camp Hancock**.

The **Chateau de Mores**, **De Mores Memorial Park**, and **Chimney Park** commemorate the entrepreneurial efforts of a French nobleman who operated a cattle ranch and beef packing plant at Medora, Dakota Territory, in the 1880s. The **Elkhorn Ranch**, owned by Theodore Roosevelt, who later became the twenty-sixth president of the United States, is another cattle-ranching enterprise in the badlands from the same time period. **Theodore Roosevelt National Park** protects the beautiful landscape and wildlife that so impressed Theodore Roosevelt in the 1880s.

North Dakota's **Former Governors' Mansion** was the first official residence for the state's governors. Built in 1884 and presently restored to its 1893 appearance, the home is open to visitors in Bismarck. Built one year earlier, in 1883, **Stutsman County Courthouse** is the oldest remaining courthouse in the state, located in Jamestown, North Dakota.

In all, North Dakota's historic sites span nearly 12,000 years and tell a variety of stories about our history and heritage. The **Pembina State Museum** features exhibits that display the fascinating history of the northeastern region of the state. Exhibits at the **North Dakota Heritage Center** cover the breadth of the region's story from the ages of dinosaurs and mastodons to the early peoples up to the modern era. More than 100,000 people visit the Heritage Center each year. We invite you to join them in experiencing our fascinating past and exciting present.

The West

▲ *State Historical Society Sites*
△ *Other Sites*

▲ Writing Rock

🛡 85

Fort Union Trading Post National Historic Site

52

2

○ WILLISTON

△▲ Ft. Buford

Theodore Roosevelt National Park North Unit △

Killdeer Mtn. Battlefield ▲

Turtle Effigy ▲

Elkhorn Ranch Buffer ▲

Knife River Indian Villages National Historic Site ▲

Ft. Clark ▲

Theodore Roosevelt National Park South Unit △

Crowley Quarry

Molander Village ▲

Chateau de Mores △

94

○ DICKINSON

MANDAN ○

Fort Abraham Lincoln State Park △

85

Sully's Heart River Corral ▲

Huff Village ▲

Ft. Rice ▲

Bismarck-Deadwood Stage Trail ▲

▲ Ft. Dilts

Medicine Rock ▲

Cannonball Stage Station ▲

Sitting Bull Burial ▲

1

⊩ Bismarck-Deadwood Stage Trail

For three years, from 1877 to 1880, a thriving stagecoach and supply line ran between Bismarck, the western terminus of the Northern Pacific Railroad, and the Black Hills gold town of Deadwood in Dakota Territory. The Bismarck-Deadwood Stage Trail Historic Marker is found by a roadside stop on the north side of Highway 21, half a mile east of Flasher. The marker located at the stop explains the history of the trail and commemorates the brief economic boom associated with the trail.

After the Custer expedition discovered gold in the Black Hills in 1874, Bismarck merchants wanted a route for shipping goods and for transporting gold seekers to the hills. In late 1876 after a treaty opened the Black Hills to Euro-Americans, the Dakota Territorial legislature quickly authorized construction of a road from Bismarck to Deadwood. In 1877 the Northern Pacific Railway Company and the Minnesota State Company formed the Northwest Express and Transportation Company to open a 240-mile trail to Deadwood.

The first stagecoaches left Bismarck on April 11, 1877, with sixty-eight passengers. Regular tri-weekly stages began May 2, 1877, and soon they were running daily. The company operated twenty-six Concord coaches and freight wagons pulled by 200 teams of horses. In addition to the freight and passenger revenue, the stage company was awarded an annual mail contract. The company erected an elaborate headquarters building in Bismarck at Main and Ninth Street and employed 175 men.

By the summer of 1878, the editor of a Denver newspaper proclaimed, "The Bismarck route from the Northern Pacific Railway is the best patronized road running into the Black Hills." A year later all of the rooms in Bismarck hotels were filled with people bound for the hills.

Stagecoaches carried passengers and freight from Bismarck to Deadwood. SHSND CO215

The transportation boom ended suddenly when the railroad reached Pierre, South Dakota. In 1880 the company moved most of its equipment to Pierre and opened an alternate line. After that the service on the Bismarck line was cut to tri-weekly trips and was soon abandoned.

All that remains to represent this flurry of activity are a few wagon ruts, such as those found near the Bismarck-Deadwood Stage Trail Historic Marker site, and the ruins of several stage stations (see **Cannonball Stage Station**).

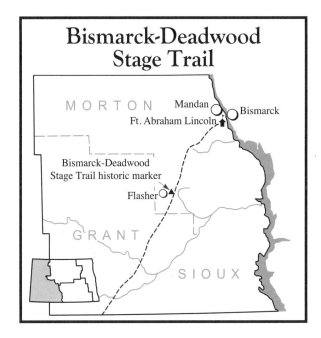

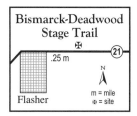

From: Flasher, Morton County (M-10):
☞ East .25 mile on ND•21 ☞ The site is marked by an aluminum plaque on the north side of ND•21.

For a list of state and national historic sites, museums, and parks nearby, see page 149.

3

⊺ Cannonball Stage Station

The Cannonball Stage Station was the fifth stop after Bismarck on the Bismarck-Deadwood Stage Trail. For a brief period from 1877 to 1880, a booming stagecoach line linked the westernmost stop of the Northern Pacific Railroad at Bismarck to the gold fields of the Black Hills. Built in 1877 by the Northwest Express and Transportation Company, the stage station overlooked the Cannonball River fifteen miles southeast of Carson, Grant County.

When the Northern Pacific Railway ended its tracks at Bismarck in 1873, the town became the collecting point for travelers heading west or south. In 1877 one of the commercial transportation modes was a stagecoach line. The Bismarck-Deadwood stage quickly gained popularity, because it ran directly to the gold fields of the Black Hills. By early summer 1877, daily stages were departing to the hills.

Whenever a stage arrived at the Cannonball Station, spent horses were replaced with fresh teams, and passengers stretched their weary bodies and ate the meager fare. Although this station was not as well equipped as the overnight stop at Cedar Creek, there was a barn and a log building. The station also served as a home to one employee.

Visitors stopping at the station today will find the remains of two dugouts (assumed to be the station building and an unknown building) and the rectangular outline of a barn. A quiet park on the east bank of the Cannonball River with a hand-pump water fountain, picnic shelters and tables, and restrooms continues the tradition of hosting travelers at Cannonball Stage Station State Historic Site.

The typical stage stop was a crude shelter with a sod roof, offering a welcome respite for travelers. SHSND A4193

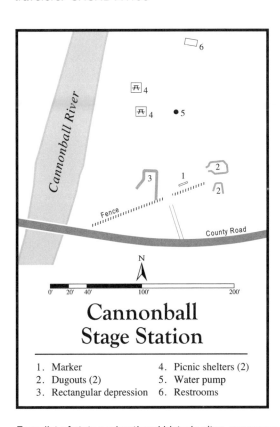

Cannonball Stage Station

1. Marker
2. Dugouts (2)
3. Rectangular depression
4. Picnic shelters (2)
5. Water pump
6. Restrooms

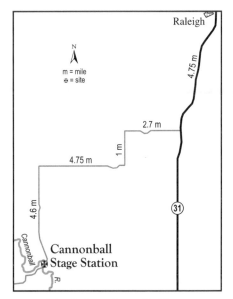

From: Raleigh, Grant County (N-10):
☞ South 4.75 miles on ND•31 ☞ West 2.7 miles on gravel road ☞ South 1 mile on gravel road ☞ West 4.75 miles on gravel road ☞ South 4.6 miles to the Cannonball River ☞ The site is marked by an aluminum plaque, two dugouts, and a depression north of the road.

For a list of state and national historic sites, museums, and parks nearby, see page 149.

 Crowley Flint Quarry

For 11,000 years American Indians dug into gravel deposits in western North Dakota seeking Knife River flint, a coffee-colored, translucent stone. Knife River flint was easily made into tools for hunting game, preparing food, and many other purposes. Several of these ancient quarry pits are preserved at Crowley Flint Quarry State Historic Site, located near Golden Valley, Mercer County.

Knife River flint is one of the most important lithic (stone) materials used by prehistoric people in North America. Its attractive color, ability to hold a sharp edge, and easy procurement made it popular. Although the only major source of this stone is in North Dakota along Knife River and Spring Creek, artifacts made from Knife River flint have been found in archeological sites as far away as Pennsylvania. The flint reached these distant locations through trade. American Indians exchanged flint for other exotic goods, such as marine shells from the Gulf of Mexico, copper from the Great Lakes, or obsidian from the Yellowstone Park area.

At Crowley Flint Quarry, rounded holes mark the locations where Knife River flint was removed by prehistoric stone quarriers. Numerous depressions, measuring nine feet across and up to three feet deep, testify to the industry of these early peoples. The first Ice Age inhabitants of the state dug shallow pits in the loose glacial gravel and removed cobbles of the prized stone. Later, American Indians had to dig deeper to find suitable flint cobbles, because much of the best material had already been removed. Early in the first century A.D., digging Knife River flint was a well-organized activity. It was the predominant lithic material in the area until it was replaced by metal tools introduced by European traders.

Although Crowley Flint Quarry has not been excavated by archeologists, archeological excavations of similar sites have produced a wealth of information about North Dakota's first natural commodity. Because Crowley Flint Quarry is surrounded by private land and lacks an access road, it currently is closed to the public.

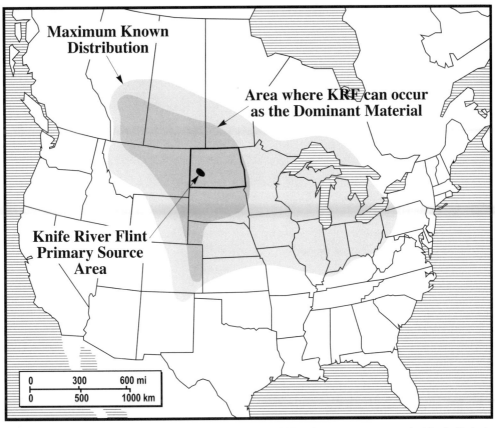

Map showing the location of the Knife River Flint (KRF) primary source area in North Dakota and the approximate maximum distribution of Knife River Flint artifacts in archeological sites in North America.

The Marquis de Mores (SHSND A0558c) and his summer home in the badlands of Dakota Territory.

⚜ De Mores State Historic Site

The 128-acre de Mores State Historic Site interprets the capitalistic enterprises of Antoine de Vallombrosa, the Marquis de Mores, a proud and visionary French nobleman. The site consists of three separate parts: the Chateau de Mores (1/8 mile west and 1/8 mile south of Medora), Chimney Park (west edge of Medora), and de Mores Memorial Park (downtown Medora).

The Marquis arrived in Dakota Territory on April 1, 1883, with exciting ambitions. The European aristocrat embarked on several innovative projects in the rugged badlands. Like other venture capitalists who were investing money in western cattle ranching, he was intent on increasing his fortune. Among his business enterprises were ranching, a meatpacking plant with refrigerated cars for shipping beef, a salmon-brokering enterprise, a stagecoach line, and a freighting company. He also founded a new town, which he called Medora in honor of his wife.

The Chateau de Mores is a twenty-six-room, two-story, frame building which served as a rustic summer home for the de Mores family from 1883 to 1886. This large ranch house rests amidst a landscape of enchanting beauty. Overlooking the Marquis's town and enterprises, the house was ready for his wife's arrival in the spring of 1884. During their short stays in Medora, elegant aristocratic furnishings, such as oriental carpets and fine china, accommodated the family and their wealthy visitors, including Theodore Roosevelt. For three summers the family lived there, traveling to New York or overseas during the winters. Among their pastimes were hunting, music, and art, common diversions of nineteenth-century aristocrats.

By 1886 the Marquis's business ventures ended, and, as a result, the family visited Medora only a few more times. Caretakers maintained the house in the owners' absence, and, for a period in the 1920s, the Vallombrosa family allowed the chateau to be used as a tourist boardinghouse. In 1936 the family donated the Medora properties to the state, with the State Historical Society of North Dakota designated as trustee. The Civilian Conservation Corps and Works Progress Administration (WPA) participated in the restoration of the chateau between 1936 and 1940, and it opened to the public as a historic site in 1941. The Chateau de Mores is presently a historic house museum containing original furnishings and personal effects of the de Mores family. The site has been listed on the National Register of Historic Places since 1975.

The Marquise de Mores.
SHSND 0042-60

In Medora the State Historical Society also maintains Chimney Park, the ruins of the Marquis's meatpacking plant. Situated on the west edge of Medora, the packing plant was part of the Marquis's most ambitious and inventive project: to supply high-quality meat to the nation's consumers quickly and economically by processing it locally and shipping it to market in refrigerated railroad boxcars. The site once contained a corral, the meatplant, a slaughterhouse, three icehouses, several outbuildings, and a railroad spur. Although the plant could process 150 beef carcasses per day, finding cattle that were fit to butcher was difficult due to the ongoing drought in the badlands. The plant closed in November 1886, a failure due to fierce competition from major Chicago-based packers, the effects of bad weather and drought, and the Marquis's inattentiveness to his business interests. When the Marquis left Medora in 1886, his plant was abandoned. The building burned in 1907. A tall, native-brick chimney still stands in silent tribute to this early attempt to capitalize on the meatpacking business.

De Mores Memorial Park in downtown Medora displays a bronze statue of the Marquis de Mores, erected in 1926. In the late 1930s, WPA efforts to improve the property included a stone wall with hand-hammered ornamental iron pickets and entrance gate that encircles the park, flagstone walkways, and landscaping with native vegetation. The project is a good example of WPA stonework and landscape architecture.

De Mores State Historic Site is open to the public daily from May 16 through September 15 and by appointment. The interpretive center near the Chateau de Mores is free to the public; there is an admission fee for guided tours of the Chateau. State Historical Society of North Dakota Foundation members and children age five and under are admitted free; school groups pay reduced admission.

Brochures describing the site are available at the site or from the State Historical Society of North Dakota. For more information, contact the Site Supervisor, De Mores State Historic Site, Box 106, Medora, North Dakota, 58645, or call (701) 623-4355.

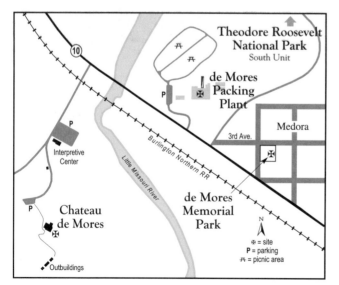

At: Medora, Billings County (K-3):

① The Chateau de Mores access road is 1.25 miles east of I-94 exit 24, south of US•10 ☞ The Interpretive Center is .3 mile south on the access road ☞ The Chateau is .6 mile south on the access road.

≠ Approaching Medora from I-94 exit 24 on US•10, the de Mores Packing Plant site access road is .5 mile east of the Little Missouri River on the north side of the road.

③ The de Mores Memorial Park is located in the southeast corner of the intersection of Main Street and 3rd Ave. in Medora

For a list of state and national historic sites, museums, and parks nearby, see page 149.

de Mores Packing Plant
(1886)

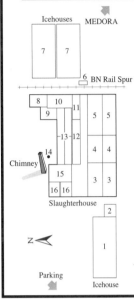

Icehouses   MEDORA

6   BN Rail Spur

Chimney

Slaughterhouse

Z

Parking

Icehouse

1. West icehouse
2. Ice elevator
3. Kill rooms
4. Coolers
5. Chill rooms
6. Salt room
7. East icehouses (2)
8. Fertilizer room
9. Cooper shop
10. Fertilizer press & small slaughterhouse
11. Office
12. Open space
13. Vats
14. Well
15. Boiler & engine room
16. Vats

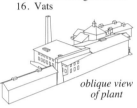

oblique view of plant

The diagram at left shows the layout of the meatpacking plant in 1886. Meatpacking operations began in October 1883. De Mores enlarged the plant in 1884, and when the new facility was completed in September 1885, it was said to be the most modern and complete for its size in the country (center photograph, ca. 1885, SHSND 0042-75). All that remains of the plant are the foundation ruins and the tall, native brick chimney, preserved as part of the De Mores State Historic Site. Pictured on the opposite page is the bronze statue of the Marquis de Mores, erected in the de Mores Memorial Park in June 1926, a gift of the Marquis's sons, Louis and Paul Vallombrosa.

11

✠ Elkhorn Ranch Buffer Zone

Flanking the north and south sides of the National Park Service's Elkhorn Ranch in the western badlands is the land owned by the state of North Dakota that provides a buffer zone for the site. At Elkhorn Ranch, the National Park Service manages the archeological remains of former president Theodore Roosevelt's home and outbuildings, including the original dugout and ruins of the horse corral, blacksmith shop, barn, other corrals, fence lines, utility shed and pen, and chicken coop. The pristine lands owned and managed by the state were originally part of Roosevelt's property and currently preserve landscapes and viewscapes around the original Elkhorn Ranch.

Theodore Roosevelt came to the area in the fall of 1883 to hunt wild game. He became interested in ranching and started a cattle venture at the Maltese Cross Ranch south of Medora. When his first year of ranching proved successful, he expanded north to the Elkhorn Ranch, which he considered his home ranch. Unfortunately, the harsh winter of 1886-1887 proved disastrous when 60 percent of his herd perished. Competition from eastern cattle raisers aggravated the situation. Roosevelt also had less time to devote to his ranching operations as he gained prominence in politics. Although he revisited the Elkhorn Ranch, he finally sold his holdings in 1898. He became president of the United States in 1901.

Elkhorn Ranch lies midway between the north and south units of Theodore Roosevelt National Park and is located thirty-five miles north of Medora on the west bank of the Little Missouri River. It is currently accessible only by a rough, unpaved trail followed by a short cross-country hike on an unmarked path. A bulletin board and map that interpret the ruins of the ranch are located one-half mile into the park service property.

Visitors should check at the Medora Visitors Center, National Park Service, for access routes and road conditions before attempting to reach the ranch. For more information, contact the Superintendent, Theodore Roosevelt National Park, Box 7, Medora, North Dakota 58645, call (701) 623-4466 (south unit) or (701) 842-2333 (north unit), or visit the web site www.nps.gov/thro.

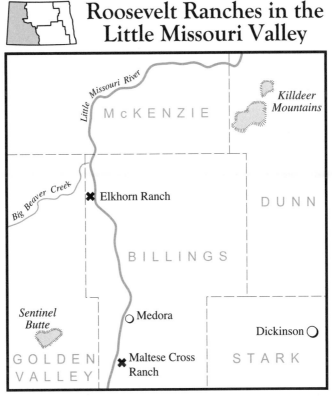

Roosevelt Ranches in the Little Missouri Valley

The view on the facing page is from a high butte west of the buffer zone.

⬆ Fort Abraham Lincoln State Park

Rich in both military and American Indian history, Fort Abraham Lincoln State Park is located seven miles south of Mandan on Highway 1806. It is perhaps best known as the home of Lt. Colonel George Armstrong Custer and the Seventh Cavalry, but long before the military post was built, this location was home to the Mandan Indian people who lived at On-A-Slant Village.

On-A-Slant Village is one of several traditional settlements in which the Mandan lived for many generations near the mouth of the Heart River, so named for its central place in the Mandan world. Recent studies indicate that On-A-Slant Village was settled in the 1500s and was occupied continuously for at least two hundred years. Lewis and Clark camped across the Missouri River from this village and recorded that the settlement was in ruins, having been abandoned about twenty-five years earlier. Lodge depressions are visible at the site, along with four reconstructed earthlodges, including a very large circular earthlodge that is intended to convey the size of a community ceremonial lodge. The lodges contain new interpretive exhibits on hunting, gardening, and children's activities. Guided tours of the lodges are available. Other interpretive features at the village include a shrine to Lone Man, a drying rack, and a native garden. Exhibits about the life of the Mandan and the activities of the military fort are housed nearby in a stone museum constructed in the 1930s by the Civilian Conservation Corps.

In 1872 an infantry post called Fort McKeen was built on the bluffs overlooking the Missouri River and the former Mandan village. In 1873 a cavalry post was constructed on the flats along the Missouri and the combined installations were renamed Fort Abraham Lincoln. That same year, Lt. Colonel George Armstrong Custer arrived as the commander of the new post. With room for six companies of men in three barracks, seven officers' quarters, stables, granaries, commissaries, and quarters for Arikara Indian scouts and the fort's laundresses, the post housed about 1,000 people.

With Fort Abraham Lincoln as a base, Custer led surveying expeditions, in violation of the Fort Laramie Treaty of 1868, into the Yellowstone country and the Black Hills, sacred country of the Dakota (Sioux) and Cheyenne. The 1874 Black Hills Expedition confirmed the presence of gold in the Black Hills, setting in motion a flood of illegal immigration. When President Grant and his military advisers determined that 1876 would be the year to force all the free bands of Indians onto reservations, the Seventh Cavalry rode to Montana Territory where, on June 25, 1876, Custer and his men were defeated at the Little Bighorn. Custer and some of his closest friends and relatives at Fort Abraham Lincoln were among the 265 U.S. soldiers killed.

The photograph on the facing page, showing Fort Lincoln in the distance and On-A-Slant Indian Village in the lower left, is the view from the Fort McKeen infantry post. Custer's home is shown below in a ca. 1875 photo (SHSND 0260-3). The Custer home today with the Commissary, both reconstructed, are shown to the right. Photo courtesy of ND Commerce Department Tourism Division.

The home in which George and Libbie Custer lived at the fort has been reconstructed and is open for tours. From the front porch, visitors can watch the activities on Cavalry Square. Visitors can also inspect the reconstructed commissary store, granary, enlisted men's barracks, and the infantry blockhouses overlooking the Missouri Valley.

A modern campground with picnic sites and playground equipment is located in a wooded area adjacent to the Heart River. Walking trails, seasonal living history demonstrations, interpretive programs, and guided tours of the Custer home are features of the park. Other activities include shoreline fishing, horseback riding, and a snowmobile trailhead. The park is open year round. The visitor center, reconstructed historic buildings, and On-A-Slant Village are open from 9 a.m. to 7 p.m. Memorial Day through Labor Day, 9 a.m. to 5 p.m. in September, 1 to 5 p.m. in October, and by appointment the rest of the year. There is a daily park entrance fee and annual park permits are available. Additional fees are charged for campsites and for tours of the historic buildings and village. For more information, contact the North Dakota Parks and Recreation Department, 1835 Bismarck Expressway, Bismarck, North Dakota 58504, call (701) 328-5357, e-mail parkrec@state.nd.us, or go to the web site http://ndparks.com/parks/flsp.htm.

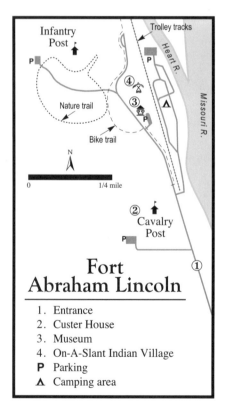

Fort Abraham Lincoln

1. Entrance
2. Custer House
3. Museum
4. On-A-Slant Indian Village
P Parking
▲ Camping area

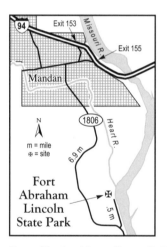

From: Mandan, Morton County (L-11):
☞ From the intersection of Main Street and 6th Ave. NE, 6.9 miles south on ND•1806 ☞ North .5 mile to park entrance.

For a list of state and national historic sites, museums, and parks nearby, see page 150.

⬧ Fort Buford

Fort Buford, located near present-day Williston, was one of a number of military posts established to protect overland and river routes used by immigrants settling the West. While it served an essential role as the sentinel on the northern plains for twenty-nine years, it is probably best remembered as the place where the famous Hunkpapa Sioux leader, Sitting Bull, surrendered in 1881.

On June 15, 1866, soldiers under the command of brevet Lieutenant Colonel William G. Rankin commenced building a new fort in Dakota Territory. It was named after the late Major General John Buford, hero of Gettysburg. By the end of November, the finished fort consisted of a 360-foot-square stockade enclosing log and adobe buildings, which was constructed to house a single company garrison.

Although historically the Fort Buford region was claimed by the Hidatsa, the Dakota (Sioux) controlled the area after the Hidatsa population was decimated by smallpox. The Dakota, angered by the establishment of the fort, attacked a work party at the sawmill on December 21, 1866. Raids continued sporadically throughout the winter. Post Surgeon James P. Kimball noted that these attacks were led by Sitting Bull (see **Sitting Bull Burial** State Historic Site).

During January, Rankin received orders that the strength of the garrison would be increased by four additional companies that would arrive in the spring. Construction of a larger fort to house the new troops began in 1867. The old stockade was partially demolished and original buildings were either remodeled or torn down. The new fort measured 999 feet by 600 feet and was enclosed on three sides by a twelve-foot stockade. Unfortunately, the buildings were constructed from handmade adobe bricks and green lumber, which caused deterioration within three years. The deplorable condition of the buildings, as well as increased Indian attacks, necessitated the construction of an expanded fort in 1871-1872. As part of the third construction phase, the post was designed to be a ten-company post but was ultimately built to house six companies.

While the fort construction was underway, the Northern Pacific Railway resumed survey activities west of the Missouri River. These Yellowstone expeditions of 1871-1873 and the Black Hills expedition of 1874, violated the Treaty of 1868. The Dakota were provoked and felt the president of the United States "must stop the railroad," because it would destroy or chase away wildlife. They would not let the invasion of their lands go unchallenged.

By late 1875, the situation had deteriorated to the point that the secretary of interior asked the secretary of war to force Indians onto their respective reservations. This action began the Sioux Wars of 1876-1879 that included the defeat of Custer at the Battle of the Little Bighorn and Sitting Bull's flight into Canada. Sitting Bull struggled to maintain his independence, but lack of game for hunting and the desire of his people to return to their relatives led him to return to Dakota Territory. Thirty-five families, 187 people in all, traveled with Sitting Bull to Fort Buford, where on July 20, 1881, the great Hunkpapa leader surrendered his Winchester .44 caliber carbine to Major D. H. Brotherton, Fort Buford's commander.

The role of the army at Fort Buford for the next fifteen years was to protect survey and construction crews of the Great Northern Railway, to prevent Indians and Métis from crossing the international boundary from Canada, and to police the area against outlaws. By 1895 the Fort Buford buildings were so dilapidated that repairs were deemed too expensive to undertake. Because the fort was no longer necessary for the mission of the army, it was abandoned on October 1, 1895.

Currently, three original buildings stand at Fort Buford State Historic Site: the stone powder magazine, the newly restored wood-frame officers' quarters, and a wood-frame officer-of-the-guard building. A modern restroom and office building and the site supervisor's home are located across the road from the museum. Although the original guardhouse is gone, its "ghost" remains. A metal framework outlines the building, showing its original size and shape while preserving the original foundation. Reconstruction of an enlisted men's baracks is ongoing.

Southwest of the museum is the fort cemetery. After the fort was abandoned, all military personnel buried at Fort Buford were disinterred and removed to the national cemetery at the Little Bighorn Battlefield National Monument in Montana. Recon-

Officers' row, with the Commanding Officer's quarters to the right, ca. 1890s.
SHSND 0474-09

structed wooden headboards mark the graves where soldiers were once interred. As far as it is known, the graves marked by civilian headstones still contain the bodies of those interred there. Nearby is a picnic area and campground.

Under construction is the Missouri-Yellowstone Confluence Interpretive Center (right), located one-half mile east of Fort Buford, overlooking the confluence of the Yellowstone and Missouri Rivers. The cen-

ter will interpret the history of the confluence area, including the Lewis and Clark Expedition's presence in the area and the history of Fort Buford. The interpretive center, scheduled to be completed in late 2003, will have permanent and temporary exhibit galleries, a meeting area, a plaza for programs and special events, and a museum store.

Fort Buford is located just off Highway 1804 about twenty-five miles southwest of Williston, Williams County. The fort is open to the public, free of charge, throughout the year; there is an admission fee for the interpretive museum. Members of the State Historical Society of North Dakota Foundation and children five and under are admitted free; school groups pay reduced admission. Brochures describing the site are available at the site or from the State Historical Society of North Dakota. For more information, contact the Site Supervisor, Fort Buford State Historic Site, R. R. 3, Box 67, Williston, North Dakota, 58801, or call (701) 572-9034.

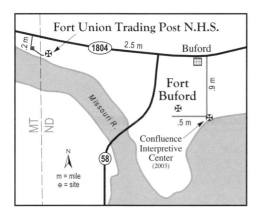

From: Buford, Williams County (F-2):
☞ South .9 mile on gravel road ☞ West .5 mile ☞ The site is north of the road.

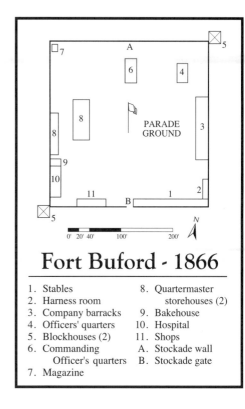

Fort Buford - 1866

1. Stables	8. Quartermaster
2. Harness room	storehouses (2)
3. Company barracks	9. Bakehouse
4. Officers' quarters	10. Hospital
5. Blockhouses (2)	11. Shops
6. Commanding	A. Stockade wall
Officer's quarters	B. Stockade gate
7. Magazine	

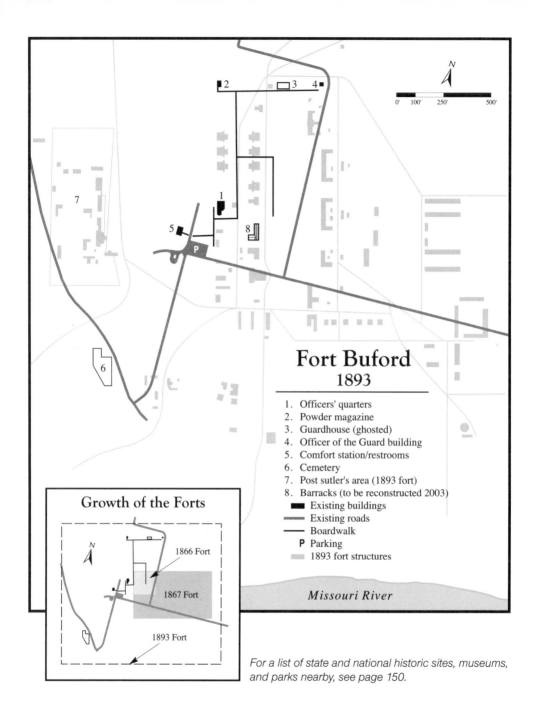

Fort Buford
1893

1. Officers' quarters
2. Powder magazine
3. Guardhouse (ghosted)
4. Officer of the Guard building
5. Comfort station/restrooms
6. Cemetery
7. Post sutler's area (1893 fort)
8. Barracks (to be reconstructed 2003)

- ◼ Existing buildings
- — Existing roads
- — Boardwalk
- **P** Parking
- ▫ 1893 fort structures

Missouri River

0' 100' 250' 500'

Growth of the Forts

1866 Fort
1867 Fort
1893 Fort

For a list of state and national historic sites, museums, and parks nearby, see page 150.

🪶 Fort Clark Trading Post

Fort Clark Trading Post State Historic Site is one of the most important archeological sites in the state because of its well-preserved record of the fur trade and of personal tragedy. More than 150 years ago, it was the scene of devastating smallpox and cholera epidemics that decimated most of the inhabitants of a Mandan and later an Arikara Indian village. The archeological remains of the large earthlodge village, cemetery, and two fur trade posts (Fort Clark Trading Post and Primeau's Post) are protected at the site, located one and one-quarter mile west of the town of Fort Clark, Mercer County.

The story of the site begins in the summer of 1822 when the Mandan built a village of earth-covered homes on the bluffs of the west bank of the Missouri River at the confluence of Chardon Creek and Clark's Creek. They called their new home *Mitu' tahakto's* (pronounced me-toot-a-hank-tosh), meaning first village or east village. The community overlooked gardens tended by the village women who grew crops of corn, beans, squash, pumpkins, and sunflowers. Tobacco was the only crop grown by men, who were primarily responsible for hunting bison and other game. After the fall harvest of these crops, the villagers moved to a winter village sheltered in the wooded Missouri river bottom. In the spring, they returned to *Mitu' tahakto's* to plant their crops.

In 1830-1831, James Kipp, an employee of American Fur Company, built Fort Clark Trading Post south of the Mandan village in hopes of enhancing trade with the Indians. The rectangular fort measured 120 feet by 160 feet and was protected by a palisade. Inside the fort were a bourgeois house, where the head trader Francis A. Chardon lived, and other fur trade buildings. Between 1834 and 1839, Chardon kept a journal of his life at Fort Clark, which records the tragic history of the site.

The first steamboat to journey to the Upper Missouri, the *Yellow Stone*, arrived at Fort Clark in 1832 and delivered 1,500 gallons of liquor and other trade goods. It returned to St. Louis carrying 100 packs of beaver pelts and bison robes from the fort. Important visitors to the site, such as artists Karl Bodmer and George Catlin and German scientist and explorer Prince Alexander Philipp Maximilian of Weid-Neuweid, also recorded life and death at the site in vivid detail.

Although steamboat traffic was important in transporting goods and visitors to the site, it also brought disease. On June 19, 1837, the steamboat *St. Peters* docked at Fort Clark carrying passengers infected with smallpox. Soon the disease swept through the Mandan village, killing about 90 percent of the inhabitants. In mid-August, at the height of the smallpox epidemic, the survivors fled to join the Hidatsa near the mouth of the Knife River, abandoning the village at Fort Clark.

Although also devastated by the 1837 epidemic, approximately 50 percent of the Mandans' neighbors, the Arikara, survived. In 1838 they moved into the abandoned Mandan village to trade at Fort Clark and to grow their crops. Tragically, an outbreak of cholera in 1851 and another of smallpox in 1856 further reduced their population. The Arikara used the village as their summer home until they moved to Star Village near Fort Berthold in 1862.

Meanwhile, another fur trade post, Primeau's Post, had been constructed on the south side of the Arikara village in 1850 by a competitor, Harvey, Primeau, and Company of St. Louis. The fort was located between Fort Clark and the Arikara village. Charles Primeau, a former employee of the American Fur Company, started the competing company.

Lithograph of a Karl Bodmer illustration of the Mandan village at Fort Clark, 1834.
SHSND CO594

After the south half of Fort Clark burned in 1860, the owners purchased Primeau's Post, which they operated until 1861. Later that year, Primeau's Post and the Arikara village were abandoned after an attack by the Dakota. Passing steamboats scavenged firewood from the abandoned fort until at least 1865.

Today Fort Clark is listed on the National Register of Historic Places and has been nominated as a National Historic Landmark. More than 2,200 surface features represent the ruins of houses, graves, storage pits, and other cultural remains. The location of houses in *Mitu' tahakto's* is indicated by a series of large, shallow, doughnut-shaped depressions. There are approximately 100 depressions marking the locations of Mandan and Arikara lodges. In the center of the village near the terrace edge is a flat, central plaza used by the Mandan for ceremonies. Later, the Arikara built a large, ceremonial lodge in the plaza. It is clearly visible as the largest earthlodge depression. Small depressions within the village mark subsurface storage pits, called cache pits, which were used for storing garden produce. Surrounding the village is a shallow fortification ditch which, combined with a palisade, protected the village from attack. Unlike palisades protecting prehistoric villages, the stockade at *Mitu' tahakto's* was outside the ditch.

Beyond the fortification ditch are large, irregular pits from which soil was dug to cover earthlodges. Also visible are several small lodge depressions. Visitors, who often came to trade, camped outside the village. The long, low ridges shown on the map are difficult to see on the ground but are believed to outline horse corrals.

At the southeastern edge of the village are the remains of Primeau's Post. Between the post and the remains of Fort Clark is a large earthlodge depression, the location of the home of Pierre Garreau. Garreau, the Arikara stepson of a French-Canadian trader, raised vegetables inside a picket fence beside his home to sell to Fort Clark personnel. The fence abuts the palisade that protected Fort Clark from attack.

Clusters of small, circular depressions and doughnut-shaped mounds near the railroad tracks mark graves. This unmarked cemetery, with approximately 800 graves, testifies to the tragedy of epidemics that nearly annihilated the occupants of the Mandan and Arikara villages.

Fort Clark is open daily May 16 through September 15. Modern restrooms, a picnic area, and an observation deck are located at the site. A self-guided tour brochure, available in the Civilian Conservation Corps kiosk on-site, interprets archeological features. Interpretive signs provide additional information. For more information, contact the Site Supervisor, Fort Clark State Historic Site, HC 2, Box 26, Center, North Dakota 58530, or call (701) 794-8832.

From: Fort Clark, Oliver County (J-10):
☞ West 1.25 miles on ND•200A ☞ North 1 mile ☞ The site is east of the road.

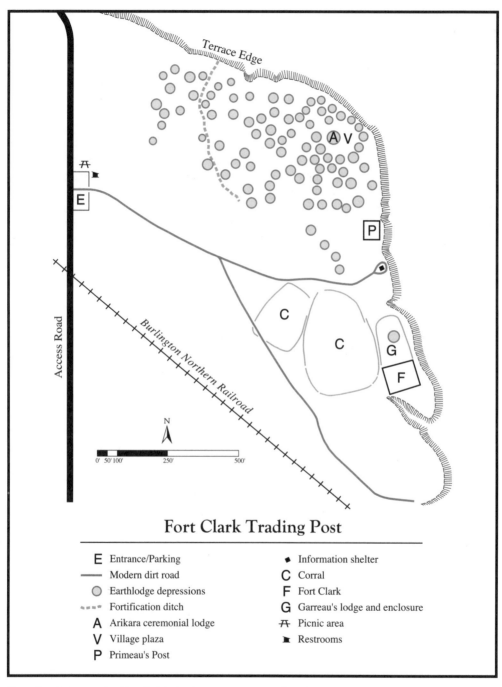

Fort Clark Trading Post

E	Entrance/Parking	♦	Information shelter
—	Modern dirt road	C	Corral
◯	Earthlodge depressions	F	Fort Clark
- - -	Fortification ditch	G	Garreau's lodge and enclosure
A	Arikara ceremonial lodge	⊼	Picnic area
V	Village plaza	�	Restrooms
P	Primeau's Post		

For a list of state and national historic sites, museums, and parks nearby, see page 150.

✦ Fort Dilts

Fort Dilts State Historic Site marks the site of a dramatic episode in settlement history where emigrants in an embattled wagon train circled their wagons and waited for rescue by the cavalry. Fort Dilts appears today much as it did more than one hundred years ago in its pristine setting eight miles northwest of Rhame, Bowman County.

On July 15, 1864, Captain James L. Fisk, U.S. Quartermaster Corps, led ninety-seven wagons out of Fort Ridgely, Minnesota, for the gold fields of western Montana and Idaho. This was a dangerous journey of more than a thousand miles during an era of increased hostilities after the Dakota Conflict of 1862 (see **Sibley and Sully Expeditions of 1863**). Fisk proposed to follow a new, shorter route across unmapped territory from Fort Rice, Dakota Territory, west to the Bighorn River, in what is now Montana.

Believing that General Sully and his army preceded them, Fisk left Fort Rice, Dakota Territory, with a small military escort of fifty convalescent soldiers. Eighty miles west of Fort Rice, Fisk discovered that General Sully's trail veered north, and he realized that the train was now reliant upon their small escort. The wagon train was attacked by Hunkpapa Sioux Indians on September 2, nearly 180 miles from the fort. In the ensuing battle, nine people from the wagon train were killed and three were seriously wounded.

During the following two days, the train moved twelve miles while constantly harassed by the Hunkpapa warriors. One member of the wagon train was wounded. Progress was slow, and soldiers had to use a howitzer to clear the way in front of the train. On September 4, the members of the wagon train found a defensive point where they could dig in until reinforcements could arrive from Fort Rice. During the next few days, the men cut sod and stacked it to a height of six and one-half feet in a defensive perimeter 300 feet in diameter. It was christened Fort Dilts by members of the wagon train in honor of Jefferson Dilts, who died from his wounds and was buried in the entrenchments. Two other soldiers, Marma D. Betts and Thomas C. Williamson (identified as "Williman" on Larned's map, see below), were also buried in the sod wall.

Lieutenant Smith and fifteen comrades rode for help, arriving at Fort Rice four days later. Early on the morning of September 20, the emigrants spotted twenty to thirty horsemen on a ridge north of camp. They were the advance party of Colonel Dill, who was a few miles behind with 400 cavalry soldiers, 400 infantrymen, and a section of artillery from Fort Rice. The Hunkpapa warriors retreated, and the sixteen-day siege came to an end. The frightened gold seekers returned to Fort Rice where the expedition disbanded.

A diary of the battle kept by William L. Larned describes the events and setting in vivid detail, and many of the features are still visible, including the sod wall, wagon ruts, graves, and an uncompleted well. Archeological excavations confirmed the historic integrity of this site. The only modern intrusions are a flagpole, a site marker, a registration box, a barbed wire fence, and an interpretive sign north of the fortification remains.

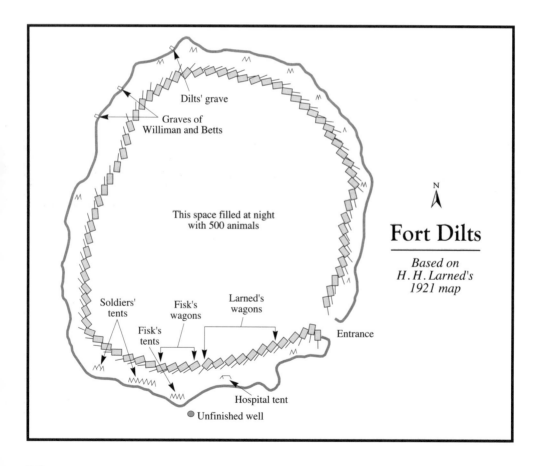

N

Fort Dilts

*Based on
H. H. Larned's
1921 map*

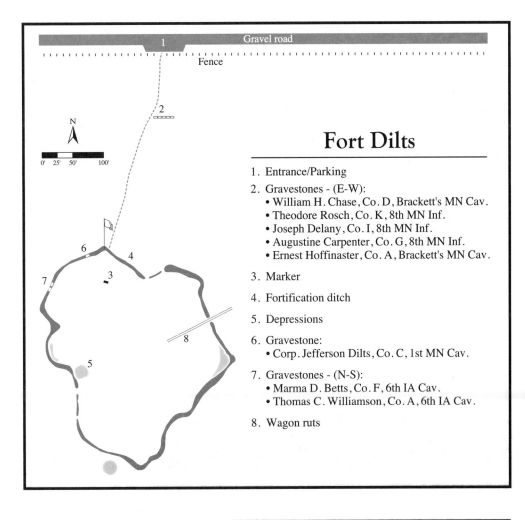

Fort Dilts

1. Entrance/Parking

2. Gravestones - (E-W):
   • William H. Chase, Co. D, Brackett's MN Cav.
   • Theodore Rosch, Co. K, 8th MN Inf.
   • Joseph Delany, Co. I, 8th MN Inf.
   • Augustine Carpenter, Co. G, 8th MN Inf.
   • Ernest Hoffinaster, Co. A, Brackett's MN Cav.

3. Marker

4. Fortification ditch

5. Depressions

6. Gravestone:
   • Corp. Jefferson Dilts, Co. C, 1st MN Cav.

7. Gravestones - (N-S):
   • Marma D. Betts, Co. F, 6th IA Cav.
   • Thomas C. Williamson, Co. A, 6th IA Cav.

8. Wagon ruts

From: Rhame, Bowman County (N-2):
☞ West 4 miles on US•12 ☞ North 2.5 miles on gravel road ☞ West 1.5 miles ☞ The site is marked by a plaque on a petrified wood marker south of the road.

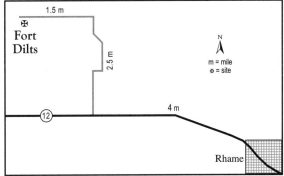

For a list of state and national historic sites, museums, and parks nearby, see page 150.

✦ Fort Rice

Fort Rice was established on July 7, 1864, by General Alfred H. Sully as a field base during his 1864 expedition. The fort was named for Brigadier General James Clay Rice of Massachusetts who was killed at the Battle of the Wilderness during the Civil War. Fort Rice was the first of a chain of forts intended to guard northern plains transportation routes, evidence of the United States government's changing policy toward these western lands, encouraging their settlement and providing protection for Euro-American settlers. Fort Rice became one of the most important military posts on the Upper Missouri River. It is located approximately thirty miles south of Mandan, Morton County.

During the summer of 1864, Indians in Dakota Territory were angry and apprehensive about the military expeditions which had severely injured area Dakota, Lakota, and Yanktonai bands of the Sioux nation the previous year (see **Sibley and Sully Expeditions of 1863**). In response, the Indians increased their attacks on northern plains transportation routes, including steamboats traveling on the Upper Missouri.

In 1864 General Sully returned to the Upper Missouri with an army of 3,500 men to punish the Sioux, to force them onto reservations, and to strengthen the peace by building military forts near the mouth of Long Lake Creek (Fort Rice), at the confluence of the Yellowstone and Missouri Rivers (eventually Fort Buford), and near the mouth of the Powder River. The army hired fifteen steamboats to transport men and supplies part of the distance and retained three steamboats to support the expedition for its four-month duration.

Sully's first action was to select a location for Fort Rice. The military reservation for the fort covered approximately 175 square miles (112,000 acres) and was established by Executive Orders of September 2, 1864, and January 22, 1867. The first structures were built by several companies of the 30th Wisconsin Infantry under Colonel Daniel J. Dill. Cottonwood logs, cut from the wooded banks of the Missouri River, formed the stockade, 510 feet by 500 feet. Two log blockhouses, each twenty feet square, guarded the northeast and the southwest corners of the stockade. The fort buildings inside the stockade were built with cottonwood logs and had sod roofs.

In the autumn of 1864, six companies of the 1st U.S. Volunteer Infantry arrived to replace the Wisconsin infantry. The "volunteers" were primarily Confederate prisoners of war, or so-called Galvanized Yankees. These prisoners enlisted in the Union Army to protect the western frontier rather than wait to be paroled or exchanged for Yankee prisoners of war or be sent north to work on government fortifications. Two companies of the similarly organized 4th U.S. Volunteers arrived as reinforcements in 1865. Upon the disbandment of the U.S. Volunteers, these units were replaced by Union volunteer troops (state militia) and after the war by troops of the "regular" army.

Life was not easy in these small frontier forts, isolated by distance and a seasonally ice-bound transportation system. During the fort's first year, eighty-one men died— thirty-seven from scurvy, twenty-four from chronic diarrhea, three of typhoid fever, ten of other diseases, and seven killed in combat. To pass the time during the first winter, the soldiers opened a theater, and from June 15 through October 9, 1865, they published their own newspaper, the *Frontier Scout*.

Men, women, and children relaxing on officers' row at Fort Rice, ca. 1870s. SHSND 0670-53

Throughout its existence, Fort Rice was a highly active military post. It served as base of operations for General Sully's First and Second Northwestern Expeditions of 1864 and 1865. In 1866-1868, important Indian councils were held at the post. The most important of these was the Great Council with various Sioux bands in July 1868. Although a key leader of the Lakota, Sitting Bull, refused to participate, Father Pierre Jean De Smet did convince Sitting Bull to allow his chief lieutenant, Gall, to attend this council. As a result of this council, area Sioux bands signed the Fort Laramie Treaty of 1868, which ended the Red Cloud War and defined the boundaries of the Great Sioux Reservation. The reservation included most of the area west of the Missouri River in present-day South Dakota.

In 1868 Fort Rice was expanded to cover an area of 864 feet by 544 feet. It was protected by a ten-foot-high log stockade on three sides and by the Missouri River on the east. Within the stockade and surrounding the parade ground were four company barracks with kitchens, seven officers' quarters, a post hospital, bakery, storehouses, library, and a powder magazine. Outside the east line of buildings were the guardhouse and post headquarters. Various other buildings stood between these buildings and the stockade, such as company sinks (privies), laundress quarters, and bathhouse. Outside the stockade were the stables, barns, corrals, blacksmith shop, Indian scouts' quarters, and the post-trader's store.

The new barracks were made of pine lumber, but all other buildings were built from locally sawn cottonwood boards. Some were insulated with homemade adobe bricks stacked between the wall studs. Clapboard siding and shingled roofs completed the improvements.

Although the fort was designed for four companies of infantry, it was later modified to accommodate several companies of the 7th U. S. Cavalry. While the average garrison was 235 men, troops ranged from a high of 357 in 1874 to a low of 61 in 1878. Throughout the history of the fort, the soldiers guarded against Indian attacks. Warriors assaulted haying and logging parties and raided the horse and cattle herds of the army and of civilian traders. These raids continued as late as 1877.

Between 1871 and 1873, Fort Rice served as the base for the First, Second, and Third Yellowstone expeditions, which escorted parties surveying the route of the Northern Pacific Railroad. Four companies of the Fort Rice contingent of the 7th Cavalry accompanied Lieutenant Colonel George A. Custer on his Black Hills expedition in 1874. Two companies of Fort Rice's 7th Cavalry troops fought in the Battle of the Little Bighorn.

The post was abandoned on November 25, 1878, after the establishment of Fort Yates on the Standing Rock Agency. In 1913 the State of North Dakota acquired Fort Rice, and in the 1940s, the Works Progress Administration (WPA) marked the foundations of many of the Fort Rice buildings.

None of the original buildings or structures remain at Fort Rice. Visitors will see depressions, foundation lines, and WPA corner markers. A brief history of the fort and a map appear on a site marker. Parking space is available, but there are no visitor services.

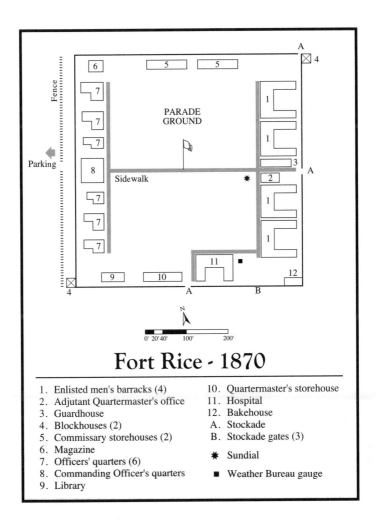

Fort Rice - 1870

1. Enlisted men's barracks (4)
2. Adjutant Quartermaster's office
3. Guardhouse
4. Blockhouses (2)
5. Commissary storehouses (2)
6. Magazine
7. Officers' quarters (6)
8. Commanding Officer's quarters
9. Library
10. Quartermaster's storehouse
11. Hospital
12. Bakehouse
A. Stockade
B. Stockade gates (3)

✳ Sundial

■ Weather Bureau gauge

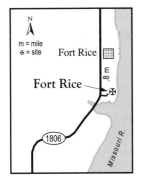

From: Fort Rice, Morton County (M-12):
☞ South .8 miles on ND•1806 ☞ The site is marked by aluminum plaques and stone building corners east of the road.

For a list of state and national historic sites, museums, and parks nearby, see page 150.

⊤ Fort Union Trading Post National Historic Site

From 1828 to 1867, Fort Union dominated the fur trade on the upper Missouri River. Built near the confluence of the Yellowstone and Missouri Rivers by John Jacob Astor's powerful American Fur Company, the post controlled the trading economy of the northern plains. Much of the fort's early success was due to Scottish-born Kenneth McKenzie, who supervised the construction of the post and served as the post's first bourgeois, or manager. Under his leadership, the fort soon became the headquarters for trading beaver furs and buffalo hides with the Assiniboine, Crow, Cree, Ojibwa, and Blackfeet Indians. Fort Union was part of a series of trading posts, including Fort Clark, constructed along the Missouri River.

Fort Union stood on a grassy plain that provided space for Indian camps during the trade. A palisade of vertical hewn boards enclosed a quadrangle 220 feet by 240 feet, and two-story stone bastions at two of the corners were used as observation posts. Employees occupied rooms in a long building on the west side of the interior. A similar building on the east side contained a retail store and storerooms for furs and other items. At the north end stood the imposing bourgeois house, and behind it, a bell tower and kitchen.

In its heyday, Fort Union employed up to 100 men, many of whom were married to Indian women and had families living with them. Starting with Kenneth McKenzie, Fort

Union witnessed a succession of outstanding bourgeois, including Alexander Culbertson and Edwin Denig. Other important members of the fort's staff were the clerks, responsible for maintaining inventories of trade goods, furs and hides, and other items. Another key group were the interpreters, who had to know several Indian languages as well as English and French. Hunters, often men of Indian and European heritage, supplied the tables with fresh meat—buffalo, elk, or deer. Traders, who sometimes were sent to Indian camps during the winter, conducted the exchange of furs for trade goods with the various tribal bands.

A wide range of visitors came to Fort Union, including adventurers, scientists, artists, and priests. One of the first visitors, artist George Catlin, arrived in 1832 on board the *Yellow Stone*, the first upper Missouri steamboat to reach the fort. Prince Maximilian of Wied, Father Pierre De Smet, John James Audubon, Karl Bodmer, and Rudolph Frederich Kurz were among other visitors who made paintings of the fort or wrote vivid accounts of life there. Some company employees, such as Edwin Denig, also engaged in scientific study.

When McKenzie established Fort Union, beaver had been in great demand for nearly three decades. By the early 1830s the demand for beaver skins began to decline as the market for tanned buffalo robes increased. Coupled with improved river transportation, the growing buffalo robe trade caused the fort to flourish. In 1837, however, the steamboat *St. Peters* arrived at Fort Union bringing smallpox with it. The disease struck the fort's employees and spread to the Assiniboine, who had little resistance to the virus. Out of the approximately 1,000 people in the band who caught the disease, only about 150 survived. The Blackfeet were also ravaged by the disease.

Fort Union in 1853, as depicted by John Mix Stanley, artist for the railroad survey expedition led by Isaac I. Stevens. SHSND C0633

By the early 1850s, when the buffalo trade was at its height, more than 100,000 buffalo robes were shipped out of Fort Union each year. Signs of coming change, however, were apparent on the upper Missouri. While buffalo herds were still immense, white civilization was beginning to encroach on the homelands of the Plains Indians. Further epidemics reduced populations and trade. The Dakota (Sioux), who had lived further downstream, began to expand into the territories of tribes trading at Fort Union. By the time the Civil War began, trade in general had declined and the post was in need of repair. After the Dakota Conflict of 1862 in Minnesota, the U.S. Army undertook campaigns against the Dakota (Sioux) that led to the establishment of Fort Buford nearby. Fort Union was acquired by the Army in 1867 and the buildings were dismantled and used to expand Fort Buford.

Reconstructed bastion.

By the 1920s both the State Historical Society of North Dakota and the Great Northern Railroad had expressed an interest in preserving and reconstructing Fort Union. The society acquired title to the property in 1938 and later passed it to the National Park Service which, between 1985 and 1991, reconstructed portions of Fort Union Trading Post to its 1851 appearance, including the walls, stone bastions, Indian trade house, and Bourgeois House.

Fort Union Trading Post National Historic Site is open year-round except for winter holidays. The facilities at the site include exhibits about life at Fort Union, a video program, a book store, restrooms, and concession machines. Hours are 8 a.m. to 8 p.m. Memorial Day weekend through Labor Day, and from 9 a.m. to 5:30 p.m. the rest of the year. For more information write the superintendent, Fort Union Trading Post NHS, 15550 HWY 1804, Williston, North Dakota 58801, call (701) 572-9083, or go to the internet site www.nps.gov/fous.

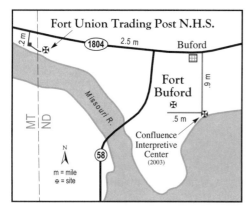

From: Buford, Williams County (F-2):
☞ 2.5 miles west on ND•1804 + South .2 mile to visitor parking lot. ☞ ♿ A.D.A. accessible parking is .2 mile east of visitor parking. A paved sidewalk leads to the site .2 mile east.

For a list of state and national historic sites, museums, and parks nearby, see page 151.

⚘ Huff Indian Village

Huff Indian Village State Historic Site was a large prehistoric village that sheltered a population of approximately 1,000 people, who were ancestral to the Mandan Indians, about A.D. 1450. It has been the focus of archeological interest because of its large size and distinctive fortification system. The village is relatively pristine, and unlike many others in the state, it has never been cultivated. Remains of collapsed rectangular dwellings, which appear as oval or rectangular sunken depressions, and a fortification ditch are preserved at the site, located about twenty miles south of Mandan and one-half mile south of Huff, Morton County. Huff Indian Village is listed on the National Register of Historic Places.

The unusual fortification that protected the village from attack featured ten bastions spaced at regular intervals providing an impressive defense of the village. The dry moat (ditch) was fifteen feet wide, between two feet and five feet deep, and had a line of outward pointing stakes mounted on its inner edge. When the ditch was constructed, excavated soil was thrown toward the inside where it formed a distinct, low ridge. A palisade of posts was mounted on the ridge, about fifteen feet from the middle of the ditch. The fortification enclosed an eight-acre rectangular area containing at least 103 house depressions, although originally it may have been more than ten acres in size with 115 houses. The east side of the site facing the river was protected by a steep bank.

Archeological excavations reveal that the houses were predominantly long, rectangular buildings. Multiple fireplaces within the houses suggest that the homes were occupied by extended families (multiple generations or close relatives) of about nine people, each with its own fireplace. The houses were roughly aligned in rows, with the entrances facing away from the river.

An exceptionally large house, located in the approximate center of the village, faced southwest toward a large, open area similar to the ceremonial plaza of historic Mandan villages. This building may have served as the village's ceremonial lodge. Archeological excavations from the building remain open, leaving conspicuous hollows showing the locations of the house entryway, central hearth, storage pits, and post holes from the building's structural framework.

From A.D. 1100 to 1400, small settlements were broadly distributed along the Missouri River and other major streams in the state. Later (A.D. 1400-1600), there were fewer villages, but they were large, heavily fortified, compact sites such as Huff. Village density was about two to four houses per acre at the earlier sites but rose to approximately twelve houses per acre at Huff, where a much larger population resided. The consolidated and highly fortified villages show that a hostile environment threatened these horticulturists, although the identity of foes of the Huff villagers is unknown. Factors for increased hostilities could have been the weakening of the small village groups by drought combined with increasing raids by nomads and, perhaps, competing downriver village groups.

By about the sixteenth century, the Mandan settlements changed from villages of long, rectangular houses, such as at Huff, to highly compact settlements of smaller, circular earthlodges, such as On-A-Slant Village at **Fort Abraham Lincoln State Park** (see **Molander Indian Village** and **Double Ditch Indian Village**). The reason for the change is unknown, but motivating factors may have been conservation of building materials, heating efficiency, and influence from the Arikara, who lived in circular earthlodges (see **Fort Clark**).

Archeologists excavated portions of the village in 1938-1939, 1959, and 1960, prior to increased erosion by Lake Oahe. In all, eleven houses and two bastions were investigated, resulting in the recovery of thousands of artifacts and, more importantly, providing scientific information about the inhabitants of this ancient site. An interpretive marker with a map stands near the entrance gate and other interpretive signs at the site provide additional information.

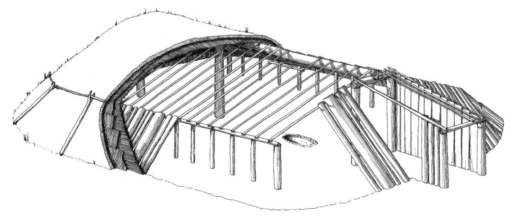

A cutaway view of a rectangular earthlodge constructed by Plains Village peoples.

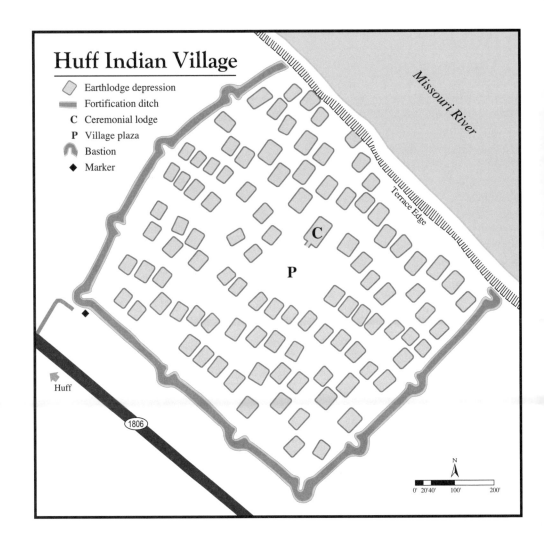

Huff Indian Village

- 🛡 Earthlodge depression
- ▬ Fortification ditch
- **C** Ceremonial lodge
- **P** Village plaza
- ⌒ Bastion
- ◆ Marker

Missouri River

Terrace Edge

C

P

Huff

1806

N

0' 20'40'   100'   200'

N

⊞ = site

Missouri R.

1806

Huff

Huff
⊞ Indian
Village

At: Huff, Morton County (L-12):
☞ The site is east of ND•1806 on the south side of the town of Huff.

For a list of state and national historic sites, museums, and parks nearby, see page 151.

↟ Killdeer Mountain Battlefield

Killdeer Mountain Battlefield State Historic Site commemorates a battle fought on July 28, 1864, between troops commanded by General Sully and a gathering of Teton, Yanktonai, and Dakota (Sioux) Indians. The army had returned to northern Dakota Territory seeking Dakota Indians, who had escaped from the 1863 Battle of Whitestone Hill (see **Whitestone Hill Battlefield**). This assault on an Indian trading village in the Killdeer Mountains was part of the military reprisals against the Sioux that followed the Dakota Conflict of 1862 in Minnesota. Many of the participants, however, were Teton, who were not involved in the Dakota Conflict. The Killdeer Mountain Battlefield is eight and one-half miles northwest of Killdeer, Dunn County.

On the afternoon of July 26, 1864, General Sully, with 2,200 troops supported by several artillery batteries, left a wagon train at the Heart River and began a march to an Indian village in the Killdeer Mountains (see **Sully's Heart River Corral**). That afternoon, military scouts fought a brief skirmish with a scouting party of Indians, but the troops pushed on.

About 11:00 a.m. on July 28, scouts raced back to the column, which had stopped for breakfast on the north side of present-day Killdeer, and told Sully that they had found an Indian camp of about 1,600 to 1,800 lodges a few miles ahead. To assure a combat-ready advance, Sully immediately rearranged the marching order of the command into a phalanx, a huge, hollow square that extended a mile and a quarter on each side. Inside the square were two batteries of artillery, transport wagons, ambulances, and the command staff. Because the terrain was too broken and rough for concerted cavalry maneuvers, much of the cavalry dismounted to fight on foot. Every fourth man took the reigns of his mount and three other horses and waited inside the square until needed.

In this formation, the column started off toward the village site. After four or five miles, the army confronted the Indians, who were arrayed across a shallow valley and along the top of low ridges to the north and the south of the valley. Stories differ about who fired the first shot, but events rapidly unfolded. As the troops drew closer, long lines of Indian warriors rode along the flanks of the phalanx circling around to the rear. Feints and counter-feints were attempted on both sides, as small skirmish lines formed and drifted away from the main column; however, the soldiers' phalanx continued to move inexorably toward the Indian encampment.

At one point, cannons were brought forward to clear onlookers from a prominent hill, which stood squarely in the line's advance. At another point, an Indian scouting party, returning to the village, threatened the supply wagons at the rear of the phalanx, until another battery was rushed back to support the harried rear line. Foot by painful foot, the soldiers advanced, and inch by inch, the Indians yielded.

As the day wore on and it became apparent that the full force of both sides were unlikely to engage in a pitched battle, Major Brackett led a cavalry charge that broke the Indian line and drove it into forested breaks in front of and beside the village. Meanwhile, a battery of cannons secured a position overlooking the village. From this vantage point, the cannons literally tore the village and the Indians' forward lines apart. The troops surrounded the village on three sides and advanced toward the center of the ever-tightening circle.

A battery of field guns, set up to the north, shelled the Indians out of the forested gullies behind the village and onto the exposed hillsides. Seeing that they no longer had any chance of repelling the troops, the Indians abandoned their village and tried to escape over the steep, rugged terrain to the rear. As their families climbed to safety, the warriors valiantly defended them until darkness silenced the guns.

The following morning, Sully left approximately 700 men at the village site to collect and destroy all abandoned materials. With the rest of his troops, he set out to find and kill the Indians who escaped attack, but he was defeated by the deep canyons and steep buttes of the badlands. Soldiers burned between 1,500 and 1,800 lodges, 200 tons of buffalo meat and dried berries, clothes and household utensils, tipi poles, travois, and piles of tanned hides. With bayonets, they punctured camp kettles, buckets, and pails. They also shot abandoned dogs.

Leaving this scene of smoldering devastation at about 4:00 p.m., the troops marched six to eight miles back along their trail. That night, Indians attacked the soldiers' picket line, killing two soldiers, Privates David La Plant and Anton Holzgen, Company D, 2nd Minnesota Cavalry. Later that night, Sergeant Isaac Winget, Company G, 6th Iowa Cavalry, was shot and killed by a nervous sentry. Although Sergeant Winget's body was never found, the other two men were buried the following day in a little valley near the scene of their deaths, and Sully's command returned to the base camp and wagon train at the Heart River.

Although the destructive force of the Battle of Killdeer Mountain was nearly as profound as that of the Battle of Whitestone Hill, the survivors still had time before the onset of winter to replace some of the their belongings. Probably the most significant outcome was the expansion of bitterness and distrust between Indians and whites on the northern plains. This battle solidified the antagonism of those Indians, especially of the Teton, who had not participated in the Dakota Conflict of 1862,

Sully's artillery battery at the Killdeer Mountain battle. SHSND 004-08

toward the encroaching whites and committed them to continued warfare, which would have dramatic consequences in the years to come.

The modern-day site bears considerable resemblance to the historic battlefield, despite modern intrusions of roads, fences, farms, and ranches. Set against the scenic backdrop of the Killdeer Mountains, a sandstone slab monument and flagpole mark part of the July 28, 1864, battlefield. Two headstones honor soldiers killed in the conflict, Sergeant George Northrup, Company C, and Private Horace Austin, Company D, Brackett's Battalion, Minnesota Cavalry. An unpaved parking lot is separated from the site by a log barrier.

Although not part of the state historic site, headstones have also been erected at the burial place of Private La Plant and Private Holzgen, a few miles from the Killdeer Mountain Battlefield.

From: Killdeer, Dunn County (I-5):
☞ North 2.2 miles on ND•22 ☞ West 5 miles on gravel road ☞ North 1 mile ☞ West 1.25 miles ☞ The site is marked by a sandstone slab monument north of the road.

For a list of state and national historic sites, museums, and parks nearby, see page 151.

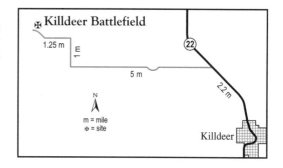

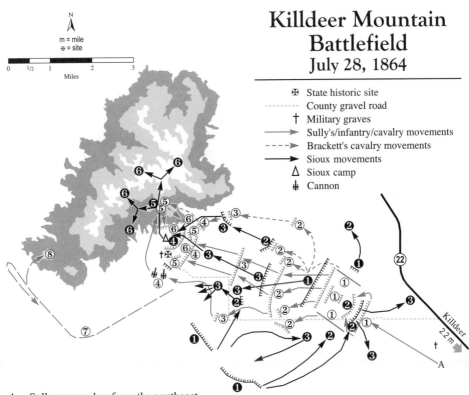

Killdeer Mountain
Battlefield
July 28, 1864

⊞   State historic site
------   County gravel road
†   Military graves
───➤   Sully's/infantry/cavalry movements
- - -➤   Brackett's cavalry movements
━━━➤   Sioux movements
△   Sioux camp
⚏   Cannon

A. Sully approaches from the southeast.
① Sully's forces form a phalanx, advance across a flat plain towards higher ground to the west.
❶ Sioux confront the phalanx on the front and flanks.
❷ Sioux attack the phalanx from the front and rear, abandon flanks.
② Rear guard of phalanx confronts Sioux; forward section of phalanx presses Sioux line back;
       Brackett's Cavalry breaks towards the northwest to flank the Sioux.
❸ Sioux abandon advance on rear guard, probe south flank; forward line retreats slowly
       towards village.
③ Sully's forces continue a steady advance; Brackett confronts Sioux at eastern foothills.
❹ Sioux retreat to village.
④ Sully's forces begin to encircle the village, artillery flanks the village from the south and
       begins shelling.
❺ Sioux begin to abandon the village.
⑤ Sully's forward line continue to envelope the village, Brackett and other forces move around
       to rear of village to cut off Sioux retreat.
❻ Sioux retreat into Killdeer Mountain ravines.
⑥ Brackett and outlying forces return to join Sully's encirclement of the village.
⑦ July 29, 1864—Sully skirts the mountain trying to cut off Sioux retreat into the badlands
       to the west—remaining troops destroy the village.
⑧ Sully's July 29th observation post.

 Knife River Indian Villages National Historic Site

Located north of the town of Stanton, the Knife River Indian Villages National Historic Site borders both sides of the Knife River directly north of its confluence with the Missouri River. For centuries this region of the upper Missouri River was a center for agricultural settlement and trade. This archeological park contains the remains of three historically important settlements established by ancestors of the modern Hidatsa people, along with more than fifty less-visible sites including older villages, trails, and a linear mound complex.

Of the three large villages, *Awatixa Xi'e* or Lower Hidatsa Village is the oldest, preserving the remains of about sixty earthlodges rebuilt many times over a period of 250 years. When the Hidatsas abandoned Lower Hidatsa Village, they eventually resettled, around 1795, at nearby *Awatixa* (also known as Sakakawea Village) and lived there in about forty lodges until 1834. Big Hidatsa Village was established by the "People of the Willows" around A.D. 1600, when this subgroup of the Hidatsa tribe moved upriver after living for a time with the Mandans at Heart River. Big Hidatsa Village is the largest settlement in the park, with visible remains of 113 earthlodges, as well as trails and mysterious linear ridges that emanate like spokes from the village.

Agriculture was the economic foundation of the Knife River people and the responsibility of the women of the tribe, who harvested much of their food from rich floodplain gardens. These women farmers raised squash, pumpkins, beans, sunflowers, and quick-maturing varieties of corn. The villagers traded their surplus produce and Knife River flint to nomadic tribes for buffalo hides, deerskins, dried meat, catlinite (pipestone), and other items in short supply. Knife River flint is one of the best materials for making stone tools. It was quarried locally and traded throughout the continental United States and Canada. The Hidatsa and Mandan, who lived at the junction of major trade routes, became middlemen in the trade. Items traded into the villages included obsidian from Wyoming; copper from the Great Lakes Region; dentalium shell from the coast; and during the 1800s, guns, horses, and metal items from the Europeans.

By the early 1800s the Knife River Indian villages had become an important market-place for British and French fur traders. The villages were also a destination for Lewis and Clark, who built their 1804-05 winter post, Fort Mandan, nearby. Toussaint Charbonneau, a French fur trader, and his wife Sakakawea, lived at what is now often called Sakakawea Village. Charbonneau was hired by Lewis and Clark at Fort Mandan to be an interpreter for the remainder of the expedition. Lewis and Clark knew that by hiring Charbonneau, his wife Sakakawea would come along with him. She proved to be a valuable asset to the expedition.

The years following the Lewis and Clark expedition brought many other traders and explorers, including Prince Maximilian of Wied and artists Karl Bodmer and George Catlin. New diseases also followed the traders to the Knife River villages and following a devastating smallpox epidemic in 1837 in which almost half the Hidatsa people and perhaps 90 percent of the residents of nearby Mandan villages died, the survivors abandoned the Knife River village sites and moved north to create a new village called Like-a-Fishhook along the Missouri River.

Lower Hidatsa Village. Courtesy of ND Commerce Department Tourism Division.

Knife River Indian Villages National Historic Site is administered by the National Park Service, U.S. Department of the Interior. A visitor center with exhibits and a bookstore is located at the site, which also features nature and historic trails through the major village sites and a reconstructed earthlodge. Hours are 7:30 a.m. to 6 p.m. (MT) Memorial Day through Labor Day and 8 a.m. to 4:30 p.m. (MT) the rest of the year. Admission is free. For more information, contact the park, P.O. Box 9, Stanton, ND 58571-0009, call (701) 745-3300, or go to the web site www.nps.gov/knri.

From: Stanton, Mercer County (I-10):
☞ North .5 mile on County Road 37.

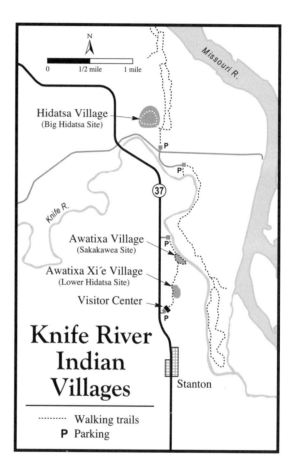

For a list of state and national historic sites, museums, and parks nearby, see page 151.

Medicine Rock

Located along the north fork of the Cannonball River, Medicine Rock State Historic Site is one of six known American Indian rock art sites in North Dakota. It is the largest of the rock art sites in the state and exhibits the greatest variety of pictures, called glyphs. Historically, the Mandan and Hidatsa Indians regarded Medicine Rock as an oracle, and it continues to be used by American Indians as a sacred site. Offerings of tobacco and cloth testify to the ongoing significance of this place as a religious shrine. Medicine Rock was a historic landmark well known to early European explorers.

The religious significance of the site was documented by Lewis and Clark in 1804, personnel of Stephen H. Long's expedition in 1819-1820, and German scientist and explorer Prince Alexander Philipp Maximilian in 1832-1834. It appears on historic maps from 1864 to 1872.

Although Meriwether Lewis and William Clark did not visit Medicine Rock, Clark's journal for February 21, 1805, states:

> The medicine-stone is the great oracle of the Mandans, and whatever it announces is believed with implicit confidence. Every spring, and on some occasions during the summer, a deputation visits the sacred spot, where there is a thick porous stone 20 feet in circumference, with a smooth surface. Having reached the place, the ceremony of smoking to it is performed by the deputies, who alternately take a whiff themselves and then present the pipe to the stone; after this they retire to an adjoining wood for the night, . . . in the morning they read the destinies of the nation in the white marks on the stone.[1]

The most graphic description of the creation and interpretation of glyphs on Medicine Rock and its importance to the Hidatsa is in notes from the S. H. Long expedition. According to the expedition, the Hidatsa called the rock *Me-ma-ho-pa* and traveled two to three days to reach it from their villages. Upon arriving, an offering was left at the stone, tobacco was smoked, and a portion of the rock was washed. The supplicant would pray nearby. When he returned to the rock,

> his presents are no longer there, and he believes them to have been accepted and carried off by the manhopa [Great Spirit] himself. Upon the part of the rock, which he had washed, he finds certain hieroglyphics traced with white clay, of which he can generally interpret the meaning . . . These representations are supposed to relate to his future for-

tune, or to that of his family or nation; he copies them off with pious care and returns to his home, to read from them to the people, the destiny of himself or of them . . . They say that an Indian, on his return from the rock, exhibited to his friends . . . the representation of a strange building, as erected near the village; . . . four months afterwards, the prediction was, as it happened, verified, and a stockade trading house was erected there, by the French trader Jessaume.[2]

Incised or pecked pictures (petroglyphs) and painted figures (pictographs) cover the sandstone outcrop at Medicine Rock. Although eroded by time and, in some cases, defaced by vandals, many of the glyphs are identifiable. A rider on horseback, turtles, bighorn sheep, bear paw, handprint and footprint, bird track, and numerous hoof prints are visible.

Access to the site is difficult and crosses private land. For access information, contact the Historic Preservation Division, State Historical Society of North Dakota, 612 East Boulevard Avenue, Bismarck, North Dakota, 58505, or call (701) 328-2666.

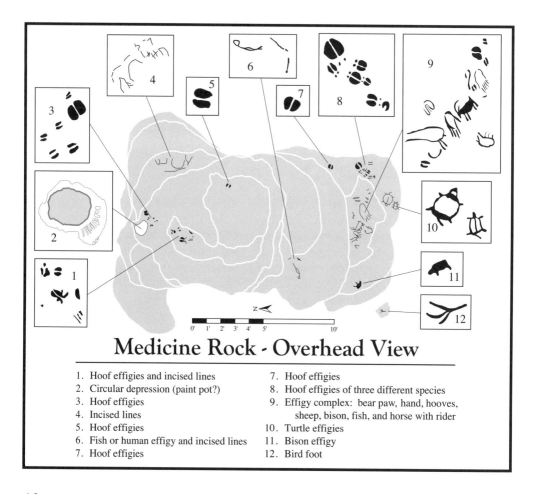

Medicine Rock - Overhead View

1. Hoof effigies and incised lines	7. Hoof effigies
2. Circular depression (paint pot?)	8. Hoof effigies of three different species
3. Hoof effigies	9. Effigy complex: bear paw, hand, hooves,
4. Incised lines	sheep, bison, fish, and horse with rider
5. Hoof effigies	10. Turtle effigies
6. Fish or human effigy and incised lines	11. Bison effigy
7. Hoof effigies	12. Bird foot

🏚 Molander Indian Village

Molander Indian Village State Historic Site is a Hidatsa earthlodge village, located about twenty miles north of Mandan, in Oliver County, on the east side of Highway 1806. According to Lewis and Clark, the Awaxawi Hidatsa Indians lived in this village overlooking the Missouri River around 1764. Their neighbors, the Mandan, lived in similar villages centered around the mouth of the Heart River. The Awaxawi people are one of three groups of Hidatsa. *Awaxawi* (pronounced Ah-WAH-ha-WEE) means "Village on the Hill."

Hidatsa Indians traditionally settled on the west side of the Missouri River in a region north of the Mandans. Hidatsa territory stretched from the hills called Square Buttes, south of the town of Price, Oliver County, west to the mouth of the Yellowstone River. Molander village is near the southern extent of this territory. The Awaxawi moved to this area from the east, arriving at Molander village in the 1700s. They lived there until the 1781-1782 smallpox epidemic killed approximately one-half of their people. The survivors moved north to Amahami Village at the mouth of the Knife River. Today, a remnant of Amahami Village lies beside the Mercer County Courthouse in Stanton.

Faint depressions at Molander village mark the locations of nearly forty houses, which were protected by a dry moat or fortification ditch. A wooden palisade stood on the inside edge of the ditch. There were six projections, called bastions, along the ditch. The bastions gave the villagers a clear view and open line of fire down the palisade walls. Each house, or earthlodge, measured forty to sixty feet in diameter and stood ten to fifteen feet high. An extended family of up to twenty people lived in each house.

Like the Mandan and Arikara, Hidatsa Indians were farmers who grew crops in nearby gardens on the Missouri River floodplain. In 1968 archeological test excavations at the site discovered seeds of flint corn (a hardy, early-ripening variety of maize), squash, beans, wild plum, wild grape, and wild cherry. Molander was a summer village occupied from spring through the fall. Each fall the inhabitants moved into a temporary winter village on the river bottoms where trees provided shelter and firewood.

There is a collapsed log cabin and stable near the eastern edge of the village. The buildings were reportedly built by an early settler around 1882 and are not related to the prehistoric site. The kiosk at the entrance to the village and the fieldstone markers were built by the Civilian Conservation Corps.

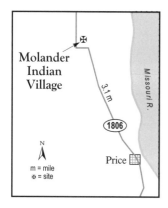

From: Price, Oliver County (J-11):
☞ North, west, and north 3.1 miles on gravel road ☞ The site is marked by a stone marker and the remains of a log structure east of the road.

For a list of state and national historic sites, museums, and parks nearby, see page 151.

Molander Indian Village

- ■ Marker
- ⌒ Bastion
- ▬ Fortification ditch
- ◯ Earthlodge depressions
- **S** Homestead stable remains
- **C** Homestead log cabin remains (1882)

Sitting Bull, in an 1883 portrait (right, SHSND A2250-2), and his burial marker at Fort Yates.

🏹 Sitting Bull Burial

On the west edge of the town of Fort Yates, Standing Rock Sioux Reservation, Sioux County, is a monument to the great Hunkpapa leader, Sitting Bull. The monument marks his original grave. Sitting Bull was an inspired leader of his people during an extremely difficult era of conflict between the American military and the native peoples of the northern plains. A historian describes him in the following:

> From the mid-nineteenth century to his death in 1890, Sitting Bull promoted the preservation of territorial isolation and cultural freedom for Indian peoples who claimed the tens of millions of acres between the Missouri River and the Rocky Mountains, and led resistance to Anglo-American frontier groups and federal policies. For this, he was revered as an invaluable leader by those he served and feared as a villain by those he opposed. For his enormous influence on the lives of all peoples in this region through more than half a century he became, to friend and foe alike, a "great man."[3]

Sitting Bull began as a leader in 1857 when the Midnight Strong Heart Society (a warrior group) and the Hunkpapa tribe made him a war chief. In the 1860s he commanded forces from several tribes resisting Euro-American intrusion up the Missouri River, and during the 1870s he was a regional leader fighting the United States Army. By 1876 Sitting Bull's followers numbered thirty thousand. When the army ordered his arrest, he and his Hunkpapa warriors, with a contingency of Brulé, Sans Arc, Miniconjou, Oglala, Cheyenne, and Blackfeet Indians, responded with a decisive victory over George Armstrong Custer at the Battle of the Little Bighorn.

The War and Interior Departments targeted Sitting Bull, and military personnel chased him throughout Montana Territory after the battle. He retreated across the border into Canada, where he and his followers were granted political asylum. Eventually, after his people began returning to their relatives south of the border, he and thirty-five families returned to Fort Buford where Sitting Bull surrendered his weapons to the fort's commander, David H. Brotherton (see **Fort Buford**).

In 1884 after living in relative obscurity at Standing Rock, Sitting Bull accepted a number of offers to appear before the non-Indian public. People were fascinated by the leader who had stopped the United States Army and had won the most famous battle of the Indian wars. A notable event was his tour with Buffalo Bill Cody's Wild West Show.

Sitting Bull was known not only for his skill as a warrior but also as a medicine man, especially during the Ghost Dance Movement. This religious movement centered around the doctrine of a Paiute holy man named Wavoka, who believed that by dancing a special dance, Indians could enter a peaceful, rich land free of white men. Furthermore, a special garment (a Ghost Dance shirt) protected the wearer from bullets. Sitting Bull sponsored Ghost Dance ceremonies at Standing Rock and Pine Ridge reservations.

Sitting Bull's influence continued to grow, and when he refused to sign the Great Sioux Agreement of 1889, the Indian Police were sent to arrest him on December 15, 1890. As he was taken from his cabin, a number of his supporters resisted, and a fight broke out. Sitting Bull, seven of his followers, and six Indian Police died in the struggle.

On December 17, 1890, army officers and the Indian Agent James McLaughlin buried Sitting Bull without ceremony in a military cemetery at Fort Yates. Some of Sitting Bull's people fled to Pine Ridge Reservation, where many died in the massacre at Wounded Knee. This massacre signaled the tragic end to the epic struggle between the Sioux and the United States Army that began with the Dakota Conflict of 1862 (see **Sibley and Sully Expeditions of 1863**).

Many years after his obscure burial, the son of Sitting Bull's brother-in-law, Clarence Gray Eagle, requested that the Sioux leader's remains be moved to Grand River, South Dakota. The request was denied by the state of North Dakota. Under the cover of darkness in April 1953, Gray Eagle led an expedition to move Sitting Bull's body. The expedition dug into the site and removed bones, which they believed to be those of the Sioux leader, and reburied them near Mobridge. Today, monuments stand in Sitting Bull's honor at both locations.

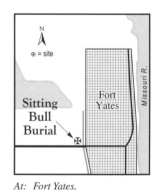

At: *Fort Yates,*
Sioux County (O-12):
☞ The site is located on the west edge of Fort Yates, north of the road, and is marked by an aluminum plaque on a fieldstone marker.

For a list of state and national historic sites, museums, and parks nearby, see page 152.

✦ Sully's Heart River Corral

On July 19, 1864, General Alfred Sully led his expedition away from the skeletal outlines of the newly established Fort Rice with a wagon train of immigrants en route to the newly discovered gold fields of Montana (see **Fort Rice**). To continue his pursuit of the Dakota (Sioux), Sully left the immigrants and a military guard behind at the Heart River. The frightened gold seekers dug rifle pits to protect the wagon train from attack. Remnants of these pits are still visible twenty miles southeast of Richardton, Stark County.

The purpose of the military expedition was to scout the Cannonball River for signs of the Dakota who had escaped from the Battle of Whitestone Hill (see **Whitestone Hill Battlefield**), but the troops were given the added responsibility of protecting the immigrant train. This angered Sully because the train's slow-moving ox-teams impeded the movements of his troops. He also resented the loss of the four hundred soldiers he felt obliged to leave behind for their protection.

Called the "Tom Holmes Expedition" after the man who had organized it, the immigrant train had 123 covered wagons drawn by teams of oxen. The wagons carried between 250 and 500 men, women, and children. A "captain-general" led the train, which was grouped into six divisions, each under its own wagonmaster. A "court" had been elected to deal with any legal matters, and a sheriff, postmaster, and a chaplain served other communal needs.

As the column marched west, rumors of Indian sightings and impending dangers kept the party watchful. Eventually, the expedition's scouts reported a large encampment of Dakota at Killdeer Mountain, fifty miles north of the current route.

On the evening of July 24, the expedition reached the Heart River. Sully decided to leave the immigrant train and his own supply train beside the Heart River under the protection of a strong guard. The remainder of the expedition would march quickly to the reported Indian village before the Dakota could escape. Accordingly, July 25 was spent resting men and animals, redistributing supplies, and preparing for the march ahead.

After the departure of the troops on July 26, the people of the wagon train spent five anxious days awaiting the return of Sully's forces. First, they began to fear that a small force of Indians would decoy Sully far away so that the main force could wipe them out and capture the army's supplies. Therefore, the party crossed to the north side of the river and formed the wagons into a corral surrounded by rifle pits and entrenchments. One day the expedition's mules stampeded but were recaptured. On another occasion, nervous guards rousted the men out of their beds at about 11:00 p.m. and called them to the rifle pits where they stood watch for the rest of the night. As a final precaution, the defenders made a "cannon" by hollowing a large log and reinforcing it with iron bands. Several practice shots proved the cannon worked and all felt a bit safer.

Sully's troops fought the Dakota at Killdeer Mountain and returned to the Heart River encampment on July 31 (see **Killdeer Mountain Battlefield**). Upon their return, the troops spent two days resting while the officers wrote their battle reports and planned the next move. On August 3, Sully's expedition, troops, train and all, again started westward to complete the summer's planned campaign.

Sully's Heart River Corral State Historic Site is undeveloped and lacks a parking lot, directional signs, or any other facilities. It does feature a pristine setting and original rifle pits. A site marker sits in a pasture one-eighth mile east of the road. The rifle pits are to the north and to the east of the marker.

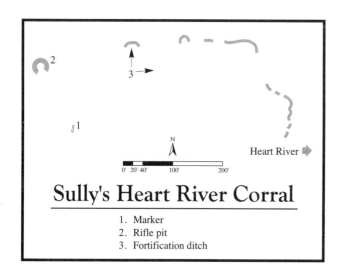

Sully's Heart River Corral

Heart River ➡

1. Marker
2. Rifle pit
3. Fortification ditch

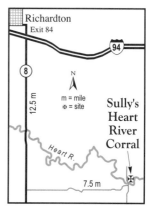

Richardson Exit 84

Sully's Heart River Corral

m = mile
✠ = site

From: I-94 exit 84 at Richardson, Stark County (K-7):

☞ South 12.5 miles on ND•8 ☞ East 7.5 miles on gravel road to the north side of the Heart River ☞ The site is marked by an aluminum plaque .25 mile east of the road.

For a list of state and national historic sites, museums, and parks nearby, see page 152.

Theodore Roosevelt (above, SHSND C1451) visited the badlands of Dakota as a young man in 1883. Right, visitors survey Painted Canyon from an overlook in the south unit of Theodore Roosevelt National Park.

↟ Theodore Roosevelt National Park

Located in the badlands of western North Dakota, Theodore Roosevelt National Park honors the twenty-sixth president for his contributions to the conservation of our nation's resources. Roosevelt first came to the badlands in September 1883 to hunt buffalo. Before returning to New York two weeks later, he entered into a partnership to raise cattle on the Maltese Cross Ranch. The next year he returned to the badlands and started a second open-range ranch, the Elkhorn. Theodore Roosevelt returned several times over the next few years to live the life of a cowboy and explorer, to invigorate his body, and to renew his spirit. During his time in the badlands, Roosevelt witnessed the virtual disappearance of some big game species and saw the grasslands almost destroyed by overgrazing. Conservation increasingly became one of Roosevelt's major concerns. During his term as president, Roosevelt founded the U.S. Forest Service, signed the Antiquities Act, and established the first federal game preserve. His conservation efforts led to the founding of the National Park Service, established to preserve and protect unspoiled places like his beloved badlands.

The North Dakota badlands provide the scenic backdrop to the park. The various layers of rock that can be seen were deposited between fifty-five and sixty million years ago in what was then a vast lowland swamp east of the young Rocky Mountains. Bentonite, the blue-gray layer of clay, can be traced to ash from ancient volcanoes. Even as these materials were being deposited, streams were cutting through the soft strata and sculpting the infinite variety of buttes, tablelands, and valleys that made up today's badlands. Fossils of ancient plants and animals are found throughout the park.

The park is also home to a great variety of living animals and plants. The bison and elk whose disappearance Roosevelt witnessed have returned and now roam the park. Herds of wild horses also range across the park. Other animals found in the park include mule and white-tailed deer, prairie dogs, and coyotes. Almost 200 species of birds have been observed, including golden and bald eagles. The best viewing hours for wildlife are early morning or late evening. The fifteen inches of precipitation each year support more than 500 different species of plants, including prairie coneflowers, prickly-pear cactus, and trees such as junipers and cottonwoods.

The park is divided into two distinctly different units. The South Unit is located north of Interstate Highway 94 and the town of Medora. Visitor centers at Medora and Painted Canyon offer exhibits, audiovisual programs, book sales, and information. The Maltese Cross Cabin, Roosevelt's first ranch home, is located adjacent to the Medora Visitor Center. A thirty-six-mile scenic loop through the park has several turnouts with interpretive signs and provides views of several prairie dog towns. The Ridgeline and Coal Vein nature trails are short, self-guided trails that interpret the geology, ecology, and history of the badlands. Other trails are popular backcountry routes. The 120-mile Maah Daah Hey Trail, open for biking, hiking, and horseback riding, connects the North and South Units of the park and offers breathtaking views. A concessionaire offers trail rides at Peaceful Valley Ranch during the summer. The Medora Visitor Center is open daily year-round, except winter holidays. The Painted Canyon Visitor Center is open daily April through October.

The North Unit has taller buttes and is heavily forested in places. It is located south of Watford City on U.S. Highway 83. The North Unit Visitor Center near the entrance to the

Advocates of the creation of a national park in North Dakota's badlands organized this 1925 camping expedition along the Little Missouri River. Photo by Russell Reid, later Superintendent of the State Historical Society. SHSND 0200-5x7-598

park provides exhibits, a store, and information about the park. It is open daily from April through September and weekends and most weekdays during the rest of the year. A fourteen-mile scenic drive through the park has turnouts with interpretive signs and spectacular views overlooking the Little Missouri River. Short self-guided nature trails interpret the badlands, coulees, and breaks. Other trails lead into the backcountry of the park.

There are four campgrounds in Theodore National Park. Camping is on a first-come, first-served basis. Group camping requires reservations. Fees are charged for camping in the campgrounds but free backcountry camping permits are available at the visitor centers. In winter, portions of the park road system in both units may be closed. Information about interpretive programs during the summer can be obtained at the visitor centers.

For further information, contact Theodore Roosevelt National Park, Box 7, Medora, ND 58654, call (701) 623-4466 (South Unit) or (701) 842-2333 (North Unit), e-mail THRO_interpretation@nps.gov, or go to the web site www.nps.gov/thro.

Hiking badlands trails and visiting Roosevelt's original Elkhorn Ranch cabin, now located near the entrance to the south unit, are among the many attractions of the park.
Courtesy of ND Commerce Department Tourism Division.

North Unit — From: Watford City, McKenzie County (G-4):
☞ South 15 miles on US•85 ☞ West 1 mile to park entrance and Visitor Center.
South Unit — At: Medora, Billings County (K-3):
☞ Access road to T.R. park entrance is at the north side of the Intersection of 3rd Avenue and ND•10.

For a list of state and national historic sites, museums, and parks nearby, see page 152.

☜ Turtle Effigy

Near Golden Valley, Mercer County, there is a turtle effigy on the edge of a high ridge. This effigy is an animal shape formed by arranging stones in a pattern. The turtle feature measures twenty-one feet from head to tail and eleven and one-half feet from side to side. Ninety-five stones are incorporated into the body, which has six appendages: four legs, a head, and a tail. The head is formed from a dense concentration of stones, but the remainder of the body is outlined by a single course of rocks.

Other prehistoric rock figures have been found on the northern plains. The outlines include human figures, snakes, geometric patterns, medicine wheels (radiating spokes within a circle), bison, birds, parallel or single boulder lines, connecting lines, triangles, crosses, and oblong or elliptical enclosures. These sites are found in Alberta, Manitoba, Saskatchewan, North Dakota, and South Dakota. Similar turtles in our region have been recorded at Cross Ranch, near Sanger, Oliver County; along the Beulah Trench north of Beulah, Mercer County; northwest of Williston, Williams County; near Ludlow Cave, South Dakota; and on Snake Butte, north of Pierre, South Dakota. Although the actual dates of construction of most of these rock outlines are unknown, the degree of sod cover and the amount of lichen growth on the rocks are clues to their age. The clues suggest that the turtle effigy is at least several hundred years old.

The tribal affiliation of the creators of many of these turtle effigies is unknown. Some tribes, however, such as the Ojibwa, Blackfoot, Dakota (Sioux), Mandan, and

Hidatsa, recognize the importance of the turtle in their religious beliefs and hunting ceremonies. Alfred Bowers, an anthropologist who worked with the Mandan and Hidatsa, attributed many of the turtle effigies to members of these two tribes. He reported that the turtle was used in bison-hunting ceremonies:

> The turtle is also associated with the buffalo on other occasions. Throughout Hidatsa hunting territory are numerous turtle effigies arranged from boulders and situated on high hills with the head pointed toward the river . . . Nearby are piles of stones on which individual offerings are made to clear the fogs so that the buffalo could be found.[4]

Turtle and other effigies are rare and fragile resources. Vehicle traffic, unauthorized digging, souvenir collection, and cultivation have destroyed many of these sites.

As yet there is no access road to the Turtle Effigy State Historic Site, which was donated to the state in 1993. For access information, contact the Historic Preservation Division, State Historical Society of North Dakota, 612 East Boulevard Avenue, Bismarck, North Dakota, 58505, or call (701) 328-2666.

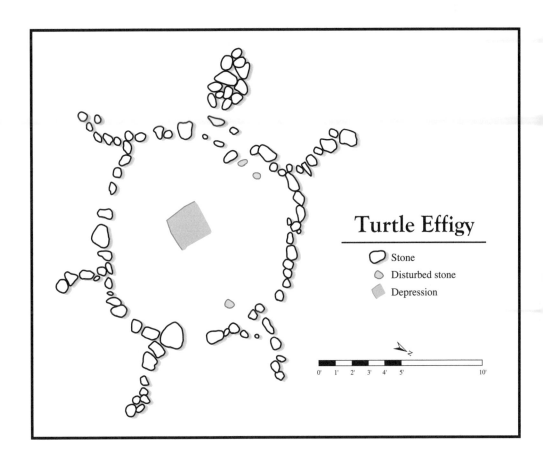

Turtle Effigy

Stone
Disturbed stone
Depression

0' 1' 2' 3' 4' 5'   10'

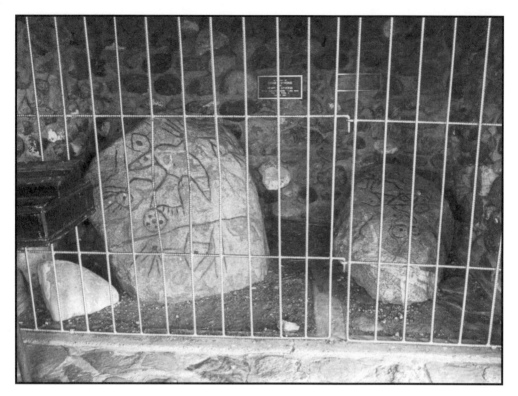

⚜ Writing Rock

Two granite boulders inscribed with thunderbird figures are exhibited at Writing Rock State Historic Site north of Grenora in Williams County. The designs on the rocks are clearly American Indian, despite unfounded speculation attributing the origins of the "mysterious carvings" to Vikings, Chinese, or others. Similar rock art sites are found in Roch Percée and Kamsack, Saskatchewan; Long-view and Writing-on-Stone Provincial Park, Alberta; Pictograph Cave near Billings, Montana; Dinwoody, Wyoming; Ludlow Cave, South Dakota; and at numerous archeological sites in the upper midwestern United States.

Thunderbirds, mythological creatures responsible for lightning and thunder, are central to stories told by Algonquian and Siouan-speaking tribes. Many Plains Indians such as Plains Cree, Plains Ojibwa, Gros Ventre, Crow, Dakota (Sioux), Mandan, and Hidatsa used thunderbirds in their art. The design appears on prehistoric artifacts such as shell and bone pendants and pottery, as well as on rock art. Most of these artifacts on the northern plains date from A.D. 1000 to A.D. 1700.

The larger of the two granite boulders measures four and one-half feet high and four feet wide. A massive, flying bird surrounded by interconnected lines and circles covers the flattest side of the boulder. The second, smaller rock is three and one-half feet long, two feet wide, and one and one-half feet high. It displays a smaller, flying bird connected to circles and abstract lines. A second bird, which is missing its head, flies above the other designs. All of the motifs were pecked by pounding a hard rock against the boulders or were ground into the surfaces.

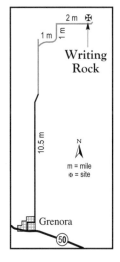

The smaller rock was originally located some distance from the larger one and was once removed from the site but later returned. Today, the two boulders are enclosed in a shelter and protected by iron bars at the historic site. Recreational facilities at the historic site include picnic tables in a grove of trees, picnic shelters, a building with a kitchen, fireplace, playground equipment, restrooms, and a parking lot.

From: Grenora, Williams County (C-2):
☞ North 10.5 miles on asphalt/gravel road ☞ East 1 mile on gravel road ☞ North 1 mile ☞ East 2 miles ☞ The site is marked by two pictograph boulders in a shelter at the end of the road.

For a list of state and national historic sites, museums, and parks nearby, see page 152.

Prairies
& Coteaus

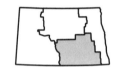

▲ *State Historical Society Sites*

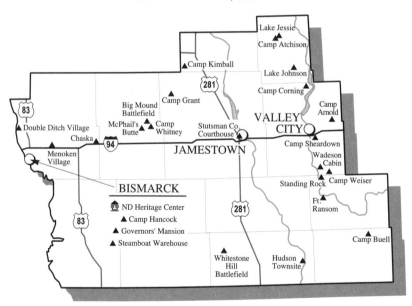

Lake Jessie
▲ Camp Atchison

▲ Camp Kimball

Lake Johnson
▲

Camp Corning

Big Mound
Battlefield   ▲ Camp Grant   Camp
Arnold ▲
McPhail's ▲ ▲ Camp   VALLEY
Butte   Whitney   Stutsman Co.   CITY
Chaska   Courthouse
▲ Double Ditch Village   ▲ Camp Sheardown
                    JAMESTOWN   Wadeson
Menoken   Cabin ▲
Village   Standing Rock ▲ Camp Weiser
                                      ▲
BISMARCK   Ft.
🏛 ND Heritage Center   Ransom
▲ Camp Hancock
▲ Governors' Mansion   Camp Buell ▲
▲ Steamboat Warehouse
                 Whitestone   Hudson ▲
                 Hill   Townsite
                 Battlefield

✦ Sibley and Sully Expeditions of 1863

The Dakota Conflict (historically called the "Minnesota Uprising") is classified by some historians as part of the U.S. Civil War, by others as an introductory phase of the Indian wars on the northern plains. It began on August 18, 1862, when Mdewakanton and Wahpekute Dakota (Sioux) Indian factions, led by Chief Little Crow, initiated a massive and bloody attack against white settlers living in southern Minnesota. The Dakota, frustrated by years of discontent, suspicion, and accumulated grievances against white settlers, were further angered when promised annuity goods and cash due from the United States government at the end of June were delayed. Fearing starvation after a poor harvest, the Indians attacked many isolated farms, several settlements, and Fort Ridgely along the Minnesota River in southwestern Minnesota, killing between 450 and 800 settlers and soldiers, while suffering the loss of about 21 of their own people. Indian-white warfare continued sporadically on the northern plains until the tragic Wounded Knee massacre in 1890.

Although approximately 40,000 white settlers fled during the initial stages of the conflict, within a few days, locally raised militia began quelling the uprising. Because Minnesota and the rest of the nation had been embroiled in the Civil War for sixteen months, "regular" U.S. troops were not available for frontier service. The available state militia troops were mostly young, inexperienced, poorly armed men, and lacking in numbers. In fact, when Fort Ridgely was attacked, it was under the command of nineteen-year-old Lieutenant Gere, who had the mumps. However, at Birch Coulee and again at Wood Lake, these soldiers under the command of Colonel Henry Hastings Sibley won significant battles, ending the fighting and raiding in Minnesota.

As the military arrested suspected perpetrators, many Dakota, fearing retaliation, fled to other areas. Of the nearly 400 Indians who were tried by a military tribunal for their alleged participation in the conflict, 308 were sentenced to hang. President Abraham Lincoln commuted many of the death sentences, but 38 of those convicted were hanged at Mankato, Minnesota, on December 26, 1862.

It was reported that Little Crow, a principal leader of the conflict, and Inkpaduta, an outlawed Wahpekute chief, had retreated to the vicinity of Devils Lake in Dakota Territory. Many Minnesotans wanted retribution or believed that future hostilities could be prevented only if stern measures were taken. General John Pope, recently appointed commander of the new Military Department of the Northwest, devised a plan to trap the enemy Dakota (Sioux) in Dakota Territory.

The plan called for one army to march from Minnesota to the Devils Lake area, fighting with Dakota along the way, or pushing them westward toward the Missouri River. Meanwhile, a second army would advance northward along the Missouri, preventing escape across the river. Those caught between the two armies would either be captured or killed. The two armies were scheduled to rendezvous on July 25, 1863, at the Missouri River, where the generals could determine further action.

General Sibley, who displayed outstanding leadership as a colonel of volunteers during the conflict, was appointed to lead the Minnesota arm of the joint campaign. He was a veteran fur trader, and later became governor of Minnesota. General Alfred Sully, a West Point graduate experienced in Indian campaigns, was eventually chosen to command the second army. Eighteen of the state historic sites in this book relate directly to this military campaign, and the individual significance of each one is described more fully elsewhere.

Sibley's army, although starting a little later than planned, reached Dakota Territory near Big Stone Lake on June 24, 1863. They entered present-day North Dakota on July 2 southeast of Lake Tewaukon and headed northwest toward Devils Lake (see **Camp Buell**, **Camp Weiser**, **Camp Sheardown**, and **Camp Corning**). By July 17 Sibley had learned that the Dakota had left the Devils Lake area and were moving toward the Missouri River. In order to increase his army's mobility, Sibley deposited unneeded baggage, surplus supplies, and disabled men and animals in fortified Camp Atchison and continued the chase at a faster pace (see **Camp Atchison**, **Camp Kimball**, and **Camp Grant**).

After fighting battles on July 24 at Big Mound (see **Big Mound Battlefield** and **McPhail's Butte Overlook**), July 26 at Dead Buffalo Lake, and July 28 at Stony Lake, Sibley pursued the Dakota to the Missouri (see **Camp Whitney**). He fought another engagement with the Indian warriors, as their families escaped across the river. After waiting two more days in hopes of a rendezvous with General Sully's troops, Sibley (see **Chaska [Camp Banks]**), his command short of food and his men exhausted, returned to Camp Atchison. On August 12, 1863, they left Camp Atchison and headed home to Minnesota (see **Camp Arnold**, **Buffalo Creek**, and **Maple Creek Crossing**).

While General Sibley waited for General Sully at the Missouri River, Sully waited for his steamboats at Fort Pierre (at present-day Pierre, South Dakota). Sully's arm of the campaign was plagued by a succession of delays. The first occurred when the expedition's original commander, General John Cook, was replaced by Sully during the campaign's critical planning phase. Cook, as commander of the District of Dakota, had failed to respond decisively to the Dakota Conflict and was removed because of public outcry against his appointment. To make matters worse, the Second Nebraska Cavalry, a major component of the command, arrived late at Sioux City.

Unquestionably, however, the biggest factor in the command's late departure was a prolonged drought that prevented the expedition's steamboats from moving on the uncommonly low water levels of the Missouri River. On the July 25 rendezvous date, Sully's troops had just arrived at Fort Pierre and were three weeks ahead of the steamboats. In mid-August, Sully, desperate to advance, loaded the available supplies onto wagons and marched overland toward Devils Lake. This army moved with rations adequate for a mere twenty-three days.

In late August, long after Sibley had departed for Minnesota, Sully's command reached Long Lake, southeast of present-day Bismarck. Realizing that he had missed Sibley, Sully turned his command east toward the James River, still hoping to catch up with the Dakota. Captured informants reported that the Dakota had escaped Sibley's army by crossing the Missouri but had returned after Sibley departed and had moved eastward to hunt buffalo for winter provisions.

On September 3, 1863, a scouting party discovered an Indian village near Whitestone Hill. The army scouts stalled the Indians' escape long enough for Sully to bring his main force into battle position. The Battle of Whitestone Hill is considered to be the most fiercely fought battle between whites and Indians in North Dakota. Twenty-three soldiers and an estimated two hundred Indians, including many women and children, died. Another 158 Indians were captured and all of the Indians' food, shelter, tools, weapons, and transportation were destroyed, leaving the survivors destitute in the face of the coming winter (see **Whitestone Hill Battlefield**). With his mission partially accomplished, Sully and his men returned to Sioux City at the end of the 1863 campaign. Sully would return the following year. For information about the Sully expedition of 1864, see **Fort Rice, Sully's Heart River Corral**, and **Killdeer Mountain Battlefield**.

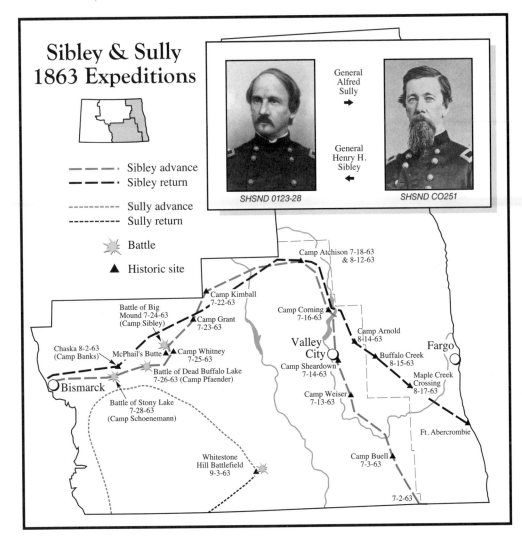

Sibley & Sully 1863 Expeditions

General Alfred Sully ➡

General Henry H. Sibley ⬅

SHSND 0123-28   SHSND CO251

— ⸱ — ⸱ — Sibley advance
— ▪ — ▪ — Sibley return

--------- Sully advance
----------- Sully return

✳ Battle

▲ Historic site

Camp Atchison 7-18-63 & 8-12-63

Camp Kimball 7-22-63

Battle of Big Mound 7-24-63 (Camp Sibley)

Camp Grant 7-23-63

Camp Corning 7-16-63

Camp Arnold 8-14-63

Valley City

Fargo

Chaska 8-2-63 (Camp Banks)

McPhail's Butte ▲ ▲ Camp Whitney 7-25-63

Buffalo Creek 8-15-63

Battle of Dead Buffalo Lake 7-26-63 (Camp Pfaender)

Camp Sheardown 7-14-63

Maple Creek Crossing 8-17-63

Bismarck

Camp Weiser 7-13-63

Battle of Stony Lake 7-28-63 (Camp Schoenemann)

Ft. Abercrombie

Whitestone Hill Battlefield 9-3-63

Camp Buell 7-3-63

7-2-63

♠ Big Mound Battlefield

The Big Mound Battlefield State Historic Site marks the hilltop where Dr. Josiah S. Weiser, chief surgeon, 1st Regiment of the Minnesota Mounted Rangers, was shot and killed on July 24, 1863. This shooting sparked the Battle of Big Mound, the first major battle fought in Dakota Territory between General Henry H. Sibley's Minnesota volunteers and a group of Dakota (Sioux) Indians (see **Sibley and Sully Expeditions of 1863**). This historic site lies ten miles north and east of Tappen, Kidder County.

The day of the battle, the column left Camp Grant and marched southwest across the rough hills of the Missouri Coteau. Around noon, scouts informed General Sibley that there were many Indians a few miles away. As the soldiers reached the edge of a large plateau and dropped down into a little valley, Indians were visible to the east, south, and west. Sibley ordered the troops to set up camp (later named Camp Sibley) and to prepare trenches and breastworks (temporary fortifications) for defense.

Some of the scouts took up a position some four hundred yards south of the main camp, where they were approached by Dakota Indians who asked to parley with General Sibley. Dr. Weiser spoke Dakota and was assisting in the discussions when he was shot by one of the Indians. Both parties scurried for cover while exchanging gunfire and retreating to defensible positions.

The barrage alerted the troops who were setting up camp, and they formed into battle lines. Heavy fighting broke out in a large ravine running from the top of the surrounding plateau down to the campsite. Sibley, recognizing the challenge of defeating Indians concealed by natural cover in the ravine, moved up the hillside on the east

In the photograph on the facing page, Big Mound, the high point where Sibley positioned his artillery, is indicated by an arrow. Harper's Weekly *published this sketch of Sibley's forces pursuing the Dakota at Big Mound.* Harper's Weekly, *September 12, 1863.*

side of the ravine to establish a command post on high ground, accompanied by a battery of six-pound field cannons. From several progressively higher gun positions, the artillery shelled Indians concealed in the ravine, until the pressure of the artillery and advancing infantry forced the Indians to retreat toward the top of the plateau.

Meanwhile, on the eastern side of the battlefield, the Sixth Minnesota Infantry was advancing uphill against lighter opposition. When they topped the bluff line, they turned south driving the Indians before them. On the west, McPhail's Rangers circled west out of Camp Sibley, cutting off attack from the exposed side of the camp. Wheeling to the left (south), the cavalry established an effective blockade preventing the Indians from slipping off the plateau to the west. In concert, the Seventh Infantry, having gained the top of the plateau to the south, commenced wheeling to the right, sandwiching the Indians between themselves and McPhail on the west (see **McPhail's Butte Overlook**).

More than one hundred years later, the battlefield is now quiet farmland with scant evidence of the conflict. The place where Dr. Weiser was killed is marked by a stone fence and granite headstone mounted on a boulder.

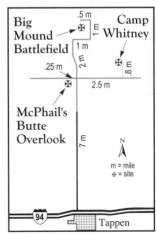

From: Tappen, Kidder County (K-15):
☞ North 9 miles on asphalt/gravel road ☞ East 1 mile on gravel road
☞ North 1 mile ☞ West .5 mile ☞ The site is marked by a polished granite marker .15 mile south on a trail atop a small hill.

For a list of state and national historic sites, museums, and parks nearby, see page 153.

Big Mound Battlefield
July 24, 1863

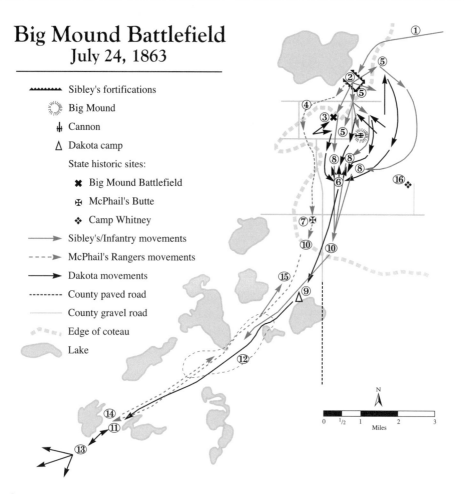

Legend:

- ▲▲▲▲ Sibley's fortifications
- Big Mound
- Cannon
- △ Dakota camp

State historic sites:

- ✖ Big Mound Battlefield
- ✠ McPhail's Butte
- ❖ Camp Whitney

- → Sibley's/Infantry movements
- --→ McPhail's Rangers movements
- → Dakota movements
- ----- County paved road
- County gravel road
- Edge of coteau
- Lake

N

0   1/2   1   2   3
Miles

① Sibley's approach
② Camp fortifications
③ Initial parley ends in Dr. Weiser's death ✖
④ McPhail's Rangers swing west around the Dakota
⑤ Infantry deploys from camp/Dakota retreat
⑥ Dakota concentrate on central plateau
⑦ McPhail arrives at butte ✠ southwest of Dakota
⑧ Infantry flanks Dakota on north and northeast
⑨ Dakota retreat to village
⑩ McPhail and infantry reach edge of coteau
⑪ Dakota retreat southwest to Dead Buffalo Lake vicinity
⑫ Infantry pursues Dakota until dark— prepare to camp
⑬ Dakota reach Dead Buffalo Lake and disperse
⑭ McPhail reaches Dead Buffalo Lake and returns to temporary camp
⑮ McPhail and infantry return to original camp
⑯ Next day's camp at Camp Whitney ❖

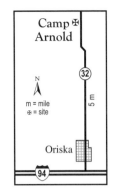

From: Oriska, Barnes County (K-21):
☞ North 5 miles on ND•32
☞ The site is marked by a pink granite marker and two white headstones west of the road.

⬆ Camp Arnold

Camp Arnold, located four miles north of Oriska, Barnes County, was the August 14, 1863, campsite used by the Sibley expedition during its return to Minnesota at the end of the summer campaign (see **Sibley and Sully Expeditions of 1863**). It was named for Regimental Adjutant Captain John K. Arnold, 7th Minnesota Infantry.

Leaving their previous campsite early in the morning on August 14, the troops marched thirteen miles, following a trail left by one of Captain James Fisk's immigrant wagon trains. Although the day was cloudy and cool, it was also windy and by noon, exhausted mules could go no further. The soldiers established a camp near the east end of Pickett Lake which, despite its poor water, supported a substantial population of muskrats.

Tired troops continued straggling into camp after a twelve-hour march. As they arrived, the men discovered that, as usual, there was no firewood and even the alternate fuel, "buffalo chips," was hard to find. However, the spirits of the troops were buoyed by the arrival of long-awaited mail and by the knowledge that they were finally on the way home.

Two soldiers, sixteen year-old James Ponsford (Company D) and twenty-two-year-old Andrew Moore (Company B), 1st Regiment, Minnesota Mounted Rangers, died in camp on August 15. Ponsford died of disease and Moore of wounds received at the Battle of Big Mound on July 24, 1863. Although the site lacks a formal marker, headstones honoring these men are visible beside Highway 32.

For a list of state and national historic sites, museums, and parks nearby, see page 153.

↟ Camp Atchison

Camp Atchison, two and one-half miles south of Binford, Griggs County, served as a major base camp and landmark for the 1863 Sibley expedition. Prior to July 17, the principal thrust of the expedition had been toward Devils Lake where alleged Indian participants of the Dakota Conflict of 1862 were rumored to be living (see **Sibley and Sully Expeditions of 1863**). On July 17, however, friendly Chippewa Indians visited General Sibley at Camp Pope and told him that the people he was pursuing had left the Devils Lake area and were fleeing for the Missouri River. Sibley decided that his army must move rapidly to catch them. To do so they needed to leave sick men, weak horses, the cattle, extra wagons, and other impediments behind.

On July 18 a nearly ideal base camp site was found on the northeastern shore of Lake Sibley. The site could be easily defended, had ample water, grass, and wood nearby, and was near known trails and landmarks, such as Lake Jessie and Devils Lake. The new camp was hurriedly established and was named for Captain Charles Atchison, the command's Ordnance and Assistant Commissary Officer. Fortified with substantial trenches and earthen breastworks, the camp was garrisoned by two companies from each of the three full infantry regiments, one company of cavalry, two cannons, plus the sick and disabled men, in all, a force of about 1,000 men.

The command suffered its first fatality that day when Private George E. Brent, a popular and respected veteran of Company D, 1st Regiment, Minnesota Mounted Rangers, was shot and killed by a second lieutenant from Company L of the same regiment. Some observers thought that the incident was accidental, but others thought it deliberate. The lieutenant was eventually arrested and held for court-martial.

On July 19 a courier from Fort Abercrombie brought mail for the troops. The spirits of the campaign were boosted with the announcement that Vicksburg, where some of these men had served only months before, had fallen to Union troops in a Mississippi campaign of the Civil War.

The following day, General Sibley and 1,450 infantry, 520 mounted rangers, 75 to 100 teamsters, pioneers and quartermaster's employees, six artillery crews, a body of scouts, about fifty wagons, and 1,000 horses and mules marched off in pursuit of the suspected enemy. While they were gone, Captain Burt led a reconnaissance to Devils Lake, where he unexpectedly captured the teenage son of Little Crow, one of the Mdewakanton Santee Dakota leaders of the previous year's conflict.

On August 10 General Sibley and his army returned to Camp Atchison. Stopping a few miles out, the men brushed and polished and broke out remaining uniform parts in order to make as impressive an entrance as possible for a command that had marched more than 300 miles on foot, fought three battles, and several skirmishes in twenty-one days. For their part, the garrison and the expedition's drum corps welcomed the returning troops with flags and music. On the morning of August 12, the troops abandoned the camp and the graves of two of their comrades, Privates George E. Brent and Samuel Wanemaker.

Camp Atchison State Historic Site bears little resemblance to the large field camp of 1863. A fieldstone monument and aluminum marker identify the site. Only a small portion of the camp is preserved, including a small segment of the original rifle pits. The largest part of the site, with the graves of two soldiers, lies on private land across Highway 1 to the west.

Harper's Weekly *published this sketch of Sibley's forces crossing the James River.* Harper's Weekly, *September 12, 1863.*

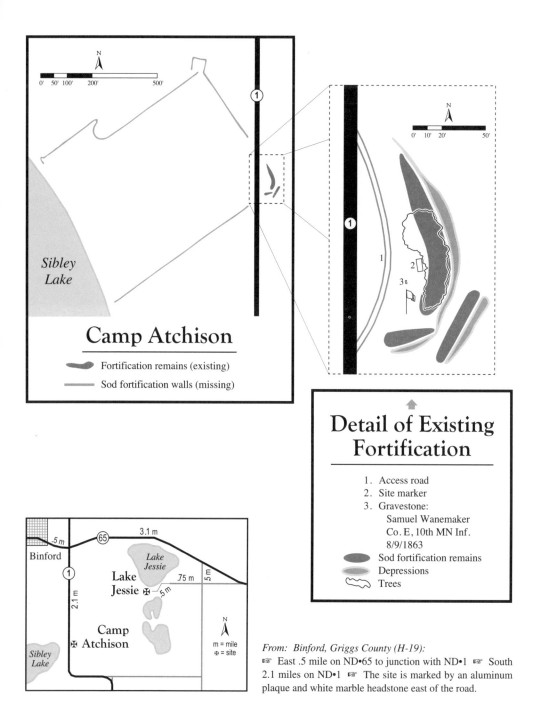

Camp Atchison

Sibley Lake

N
0' 50' 100' 200' 500'

1

⬤ Fortification remains (existing)

━━ Sod fortification walls (missing)

N
0' 10' 20' 50'

1

1

2

3

Detail of Existing Fortification

1. Access road
2. Site marker
3. Gravestone:
   Samuel Wanemaker
   Co. E, 10th MN Inf.
   8/9/1863

⬤ Sod fortification remains

⬭ Depressions

〰 Trees

Binford

65
3.1 m

.5 m

1

Lake Jessie

Lake Jessie ⊞

.75 m

5 m

.5 m

2.1 m

Camp Atchison ⊞

Sibley Lake

N

m = mile
⊞ = site

From: Binford, Griggs County (H-19):
☞ East .5 mile on ND•65 to junction with ND•1 ☞ South 2.1 miles on ND•1 ☞ The site is marked by an aluminum plaque and white marble headstone east of the road.

For a list of state and national historic sites, museums, and parks nearby, see page 153.

From: Milnor, Sargent County (N-22):
☞ West edge of Milnor on ND•13 ☞ The
site is marked by a fieldstone marker on
the north side of the road.

✝ Camp Buell

Camp Buell, the Sibley expedition's overnight campsite of July 3, 1863, was named for Major Salmon Buell, a battalion commander in the First Regiment, Minnesota Mounted Rangers (see **Sibley and Sully Expeditions of 1863**). It is located north of Highway 13 at Milnor, Sargent County.

The diaries of two men provide details of troop life. By 4:30 a.m. on July 3, the military column had left Camp Parker and was marching toward Devils Lake through withering heat, engulfing dust, and unrelenting drought. Near the middle of the day's march, the troops discovered a pleasant lake with fresh, clean water. Two of the cavalry companies splashed their way into the lake using sabers to catch fish.[5]

By afternoon, the delights of "Fish Lake" were a distant memory when the mules began to give out and one company's pet dog died in the heat. After an eighteen-mile march, Camp Buell was established near a shallow, brackish lake, with water so "green and thick" that a quart of "vegetal matter" could be skimmed off of a kettle full of the muck.[6] The men had to dig wells on the beach where sand clarified the seeping water for drinking.

As the troops arrived at Camp Buell, some men dropped out of formation and collapsed on the ground while others straggled in late into the night. The expedition's ambulances, which had been filled with exhausted men most of the day, traversed between the campsite and the route of march, picking up men too sick or weak to continue. The only consolation was that the expedition's sutler was allowed, this one night, to dispense whiskey, albeit at seventy-five cents a pint. Two years later the same site was used by the Third Illinois Cavalry, while en route from its temporary station at Fort Abercrombie to Devils Lake to participate in General Alfred Sully's 1865 expedition.

For a list of state and national historic sites, museums, and parks nearby, see page 153.

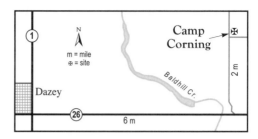

From: *Dazey, Barnes County (J-19):*
☞ East 6 miles on ND•26 ☞ North 2 miles on gravel road
☞ The site is marked by a pink and gray granite marker northeast of the intersection.

✝ Camp Corning

Camp Corning was the July 16, 1863, campground of the Sibley expedition (see **Sibley and Sully Expeditions of 1863**). The camp, named for the expedition's quartermaster, lies eight miles northeast of Dazey, Barnes County.

Before dawn that morning the troops left Camp Smith and discovered the trail left by Captain James L. Fisk's immigrant wagon train in 1862. Through the increasingly difficult terrain, the troops followed Fisk's trail, knowing that it would lead them to a good place to cross the Sheyenne River. As the troops began descending from the plains into the wooded bottom lands of the river valley, two companies of infantry were deployed as skirmishers to protect against attack. When the trail narrowed in the brush and progress slowed at the crossing, the train of wagons and soldiers formed a column nearly five miles long. As the troops waited to cross, a group of horsemen chased a small herd of elk toward the resting men. The soldiers captured one young elk and kept it as a mascot in one of the wagons.

After crossing the Sheyenne River, the expedition established Camp Corning near a small alkali lake. The brackish water was unfit for consumption. Shallow holes were dug near the lake shore to filter the water, but with only limited success. After three days without wood, the men became reconciled to using "buffalo chips" as fuel for their cooking fires. When they learned that a trench full of the dried buffalo manure cooked as quickly as bituminous coal but without the sulphur or other disagreeable fumes, this became the major fuel source.

Currently, Camp Corning State Historic Site consists of a simple granite marker flanked by a stand of pines beside a county road ditch.

For a list of state and national historic sites, museums, and parks nearby, see page 153.

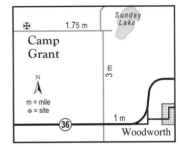

From: Woodworth, Stutsman County (J-16):
☞ West 1 mile on ND•36 ☞ North 3 miles on gravel road ☞ West 1.75 miles ☞ The site is marked by a metal plaque on a boulder north of the road.

✦ Camp Grant

Camp Grant, located six miles northwest of Woodworth, Stutsman County, commemorates the July 23, 1863, campsite used by the Sibley expedition (see **Sibley and Sully Expeditions of 1863**).

After leaving about one-third of their forces behind at Camp Atchison, the column headed by General Sibley rapidly moved toward the Missouri River, where alleged participants of the Dakota Conflict of 1862 were reportedly headed (see **Camp Atchison**). The army marched southwest, ascending the eastern slope of the Missouri Coteau, which was "very rough and rolling"[7] comprising some of "the most broken and hilly country" yet crossed,[8] and arrived at the campsite about noon.

Within three hours, Camp Grant, named for Hiram Perry Grant, Captain of Company A, Sixth Minnesota Infantry, was established by "a small, muddy, stinking pond filled with rushes of tremendous size . . ."[9] The men were allowed to hunt wild geese and ducks, and they brought a large number of waterfowl into camp that night. A fresh water spring discovered in a ravine east of the camp furnished unusually clean water. Details were assigned to gather buffalo chips to burn as cooking fuel. Each detailed man "would take three or four ramrods" and search the prairie for chips, string them on the rods until each was full and deposit the collected strings at the camp's cooking area.[10]

During the evening, a disturbance beyond the outer picket line roused the camp. Some of the men gathering buffalo chips had lingered out beyond the guard lines until it was too dark to be assigned other camp duties. To end this malingering, the pickets (guards) were ordered to prevent any latecomers from entering the camp. The stragglers "set up a howling for the Corporal of the Guard," but they "were left to howl and without their supper until well after midnight," permanently ending that ploy during this campaign.[11]

For a list of state and national historic sites, museums, and parks nearby, see page 154.

✝ Camp Hancock

Camp Hancock State Historic Site marks the location of a United States infantry post (1872-1877) and Quartermaster Depot/Signal Office (1877-1894), in present-day downtown Bismarck, at 101 West Main Street. The post was originally named Camp Greeley in 1872 in honor of Horace Greeley, editor of the *New York Tribune* and a liberal candidate for the presidency. The name, however, was short-lived. By October 7, 1873, the post was renamed Camp Hancock after the commander of the Department of Dakota.

The purpose of the post was to protect railroad supplies, equipment, and engineering crews of the Northern Pacific Railroad, as well as the citizens of Edwinton (renamed Bismarck in July of 1873). By 1883 the post had an added duty to serve as a storage station for the quartermaster's supplies bound for posts up and down the river and for points further west.

A Signal Corps "reporting station" was established at Camp Hancock in 1874. The primary mission of the U.S. Army Signal Corps was to transmit military messages. In addition, they maintained records of the nation's weather patterns. The last of the line troops were withdrawn from Camp Hancock on April 12, 1877. However, the post served the area's military needs by continuing to function as a quartermaster's depot and signal station, which required only a small staff of technical specialists.

After the post was decommissioned in 1894, the buildings were used as offices and as the director's residence for the Weather Bureau Station. After they moved in 1940, the U.S. Soil Conservation Service occupied the buildings until 1949 when fire damage forced abandonment of the main building. In May 1951 a portion of the property was deeded to the State of North Dakota with the State Historical Society acting as trustee.

In 1988 Society archeologists discovered evidence that the location was also a campsite for nomadic hunters and gatherers sometime during the Archaic period (5500 B.C.-400 B.C.). Although only a small area was excavated, it was evident that the inhabitants of the site worked locally available stones into chipped stone tools. Animal bone was smashed into small pieces and cooked for preparation of foods such as marrow (bone grease) and soup.

Today, the original Post Surgeon's quarters, which later became the Post Executive Officer's quarters, still stand on the site. The building has been enlarged and remodeled several times. This sole remaining structure from the infantry post is the oldest known building in Bismarck. Encircling the property is a stone fence constructed during the occupancy of the Bismarck Weather Bureau. Camp Hancock site also exhibits a 1909-vintage Northern Pacific locomotive, added in 1955, and St. George's Episcopal Church, which was moved to the site in 1965. The church, originally named the Church of the Bread of Life, was built in 1881 and has been restored to its original appearance.

Camp Hancock is listed on both the State Historic Sites Registry and on the National Register of Historic Places for its association with the military history of the state. The museum is free and open to the public May 16 through September 15. For more information or for specific hours, call (701) 328-2666.

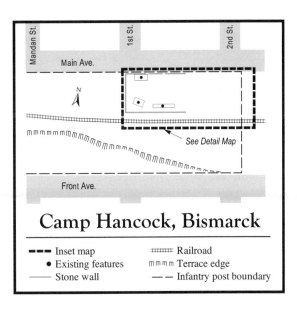

Camp Hancock, Bismarck

- - - Inset map   ⅏ Railroad
- Existing features   ⋔⋔⋔⋔ Terrace edge
——— Stone wall   — — Infantry post boundary

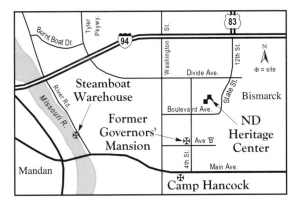

At: Bismarck, Burleigh County (L-12):
☞ 101 East Main Avenue

For a list of state and national historic sites, museums, and parks nearby, see page 154.

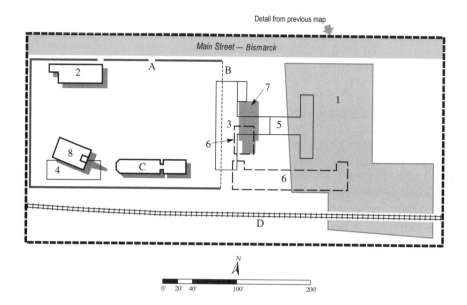

Detail from previous map

Main Street — Bismarck

N

0' 20' 40'   100'   200'

Camp Hancock - 1872 to Present

1. Camp site, August 1872.
2. Current Museum; Officers' quarters, 1872-1877; Quartermaster's office and
    signal station, 1877-1894; Weather Bureau offices, 1894-1940.
3. Original barracks and mess rooms, 1872-ca. 1875.
4. Commanding Officer's quarters, 1872-1877; residence of Quartermaster's agent,
    1877-1890s; residence of Weather Bureau station chief, 1890s-1920s.
5. Barracks addition, ca. 1875—kitchen, bakery, dispensary, hospital, laundry, and
    carpentry shop.
6. Warehouse, 1880s (2)
7. Weather Bureau station chief's residence, 1920s-1950s.
8. Church of the Bread of Life, 1880 (moved to site, 1965).

A. Stone wall, ca. 1901 (Weather Bureau).
B. Chain link fence.
C. 1909 Northern Pacific Railroad locomotive.
D. Burlington Northern Railroad (originally 1873 NP track).

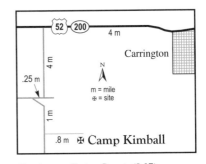

From: Carrington, Foster County (I-17):
☞ West 4 miles on ND•52 ☞ South 4 miles on gravel road ☞ West .25 mile ☞ South 1 mile ☞ East .8 mile on dirt road ☞ The site is unmarked on the south side of the road.

⬆ Camp Kimball

Camp Kimball, named for George C. Kimball, assistant quartermaster for the Sibley expedition, was the site of the expedition's encampment during the night of July 22, 1863 (see **Sibley and Sully Expeditions of 1863**). The site is nine miles southwest of Carrington, Foster County.

Early in the morning on July 22, the army was on the trail. After leaving approximately 1,000 men and unnecessary supplies behind at Camp Atchison, the reduced force rapidly marched southwesterly toward the Missouri River where the Indians they were pursuing were reportedly heading. The weather was cool and pleasant with just enough wind to blow away the dust raised by more than 2,000 men, 1,100 mules and horses, wagons, and artillery.

Along the way the column passed a site where Métis had slaughtered a herd of buffalo. A soldier's diary described the scene: "buffalo heads were lying around a few rods apart [for] as far as we could see."[12] The day's march ended northeast of a local landmark called Hawk's Nest. Camp Kimball was established beside Pipestem Creek, which had clear, cool water that the men appreciated after subsisting on brackish lake water for many weeks.

That evening some of the expedition's scouts captured a Dakota (Sioux) who turned out to be one of their own couriers. A few days earlier he had been dispatched from Camp Atchison with messages for a nearby Dakota camp. For two days he had ridden toward the place where he had last seen the camp, but could not find it because the village had moved. This supported the rumors that the Dakota had left the Devils Lake area for the Missouri River.

Today, Camp Kimball State Historic Site contains no marker, directional signs, or interpretation. The narrow plot of pasture surrounded by cultivated fields bears little resemblance to a bustling military camp.

For a list of state and national historic sites, museums, and parks nearby, see page 154.

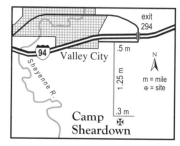

From: *Valley City, Barnes County (K-20):*
☞ South .1 mile from I-94 exit 294 to frontage road
☞ West .5 mile on asphalt road ☞ South 1.25 mile on gravel road ☞ East .3 mile ☞ The site is marked by a bronze plaque on a boulder south of the road.

↑ Camp Sheardown

A bronze marker identifies this site, named for Dr. Samuel B. Sheardown, Regimental Surgeon of the 10th Minnesota Infantry, as the July 14, 1863, campsite of the Sibley expedition (see **Sibley and Sully Expeditions of 1863**). Located three and one-half miles southeast of Valley City, the marker sits on the southern edge of a county road ditch.

Reveille sounded at 2:00 a.m. on July 14, and troops began moving out of the previous night's camp, Camp Weiser, less than two hours later. In contrast to the intolerably hot days earlier, the weather was so cold that men riding horses and wagons wore overcoats all day long.

That day they marched eighteen miles toward Devils Lake, where Chief Little Crow's band of Mdewakanton Santee Dakota were reportedly residing. One diarist noted that although they were still eighty to one hundred miles from Devils Lake, precautions were still necessary. After leaving Camp Hayes on July 12, the troops had been instructed to dig rifle pits and other fortifications each night. Nerves were becoming strained as evidenced by an incident in which a night sentry accidentally fired his rifle and set off "many ridiculous demonstrations."[13]

The day's march was considered very hard. One astute officer noted that they had passed over what was called "Bottineau's Mountain," not a rise which could be "measured by the eye" but, rather, the land rose in a "gradual ascent."

Approximately one and one-half miles east of the Sheyenne River, Camp Sheardown was established on high ground overlooking the lush river bottom, scenery thought to be "most beautiful." The soldiers' appreciation of the Sheyenne Valley was enhanced when the "Company C boys killed a fine doe elk, the meat of which was very fine."[14]

For a list of state and national historic sites, museums, and parks nearby, see page 154.

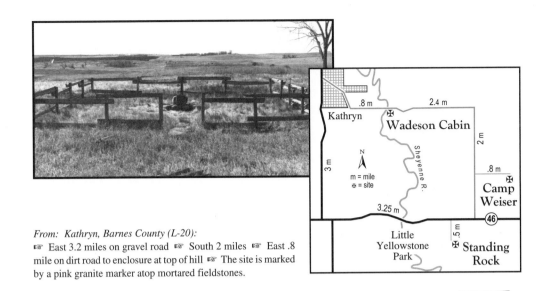

From: Kathryn, Barnes County (L-20):
☞ East 3.2 miles on gravel road ☞ South 2 miles ☞ East .8 mile on dirt road to enclosure at top of hill ☞ The site is marked by a pink granite marker atop mortared fieldstones.

✝ Camp Weiser

A small granite marker enclosed by a split rail fence identifies this site as the approximate location of the July 13 campsite of the Sibley expedition (see **Sibley and Sully Expeditions of 1863**). It was named for Regimental Surgeon Dr. Josiah Weiser, 1st Minnesota Mounted Rangers, who was later killed at the Battle of Big Mound (see **Big Mound Battlefield** and **Camp Whitney**). Camp Weiser is located six miles southeast of Kathryn, Barnes County.

On July 13, 1863, the troops arose at 2:30 a.m. to leave Camp Wharton and march northwest toward Devils Lake. Unlike the scorching days that preceded, the weather was cool and cloudy. After marching twelve miles, the leading units began making camp at about 10:00 a.m. by a beautiful cluster of freshwater lakes. The lakes, larger than many they had seen in this country, provided good protection on three sides and held an abundance of frogs, a culinary treat for the men. There were also many ducks and geese, but an order prohibiting the discharge of firearms precluded hunting waterfowl.

Late in the afternoon, the cavalry arrived in camp with the weakened horses and mules that had been left behind at previous camps to recuperate from dehydration and heat exhaustion. By 9:00 p.m. a herd of some 140 cattle that had strayed thirty miles from camp were rounded up. Finally, the camp settled down for a few hours' respite before the next day's march.

Access is limited by road conditions, and there are no visitor services or interpretation at Camp Weiser State Historic Site.

For a list of state and national historic sites, museums, and parks nearby, see page 155.

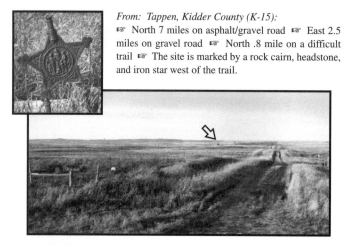

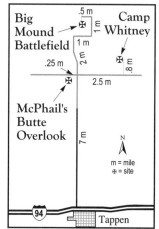

From: Tappen, Kidder County (K-15):
☞ North 7 miles on asphalt/gravel road ☞ East 2.5 miles on gravel road ☞ North .8 mile on a difficult trail ☞ The site is marked by a rock cairn, headstone, and iron star west of the trail.

Big Mound Battlefield — .5 m — Camp Whitney
1 m
.25 m — 2 m — .8 m
2.5 m

McPhail's Butte Overlook — 7 m

N

m = mile
⊞ = site

94 — Tappen

A stand of pines (arrow, above) indicates the position of Camp Whitney state historic site. An iron star (inset) marks the site.

↑ Camp Whitney

Following the Battle of Big Mound (see **Big Mound Battlefield** and **McPhail's Butte Overlook**), the Sibley expedition moved to Camp Whitney on July 25 (see **Sibley and Sully Expeditions of 1863**). There they buried Dr. Josiah S. Weiser, whose death ignited the battle. His grave, marked by a cairn and headstone, and the historic site lie approximately ten miles northeast of Tappen, Kidder County.

The morning after the battle General Sibley watched tired men straggle into Camp Sibley and decided to wait until later in the day to move to a new camp. That morning Chaska, an Indian scout, and another scout returned with the body of Lieutenant Ambrose Freeman, who was killed the previous day while hunting with George Brackett, the expedition's beef contractor. Chaska, a witness to Freeman's death, helped Brackett hide in tall grass to avoid detection by the attacking Indians. The scout was instrumental in Brackett's escape.

Before the troops left at about noon, the bodies of Lieutenant Freeman, John Murphy, and Gustaf A. Stark were buried at Camp Sibley. Private Murphy had been killed by lightning during the battle, and Private Stark died from battle wounds. The troops marched four miles to a small, muddy, rush-filled lake where they found fresh grass, but no wood. The mood of the camp was sullen, with many of the men disappointed, if not openly angry, with General Sibley's decision to rest for the day while the Indians escaped.

A small isolated part of the original campsite is preserved. Possible remnants of rifle pits and defensive earthworks are visible. Access is limited by road conditions, and there are no visitor services or interpretation.

For a list of state and national historic sites, museums, and parks nearby, see page 155.

↟ Chaska (Camp Banks)

Chaska (Camp Banks) State Historic Site memorializes Chaska, a well-respected Indian scout for the 1863 Sibley military expedition, who died under mysterious circumstances and was buried in a rifle pit at the expedition's campsite of August 2, 1863. The expedition was returning to their field base, Camp Atchison, after failing to rendezvous with General Sully's expedition (see **Sibley and Sully Expeditions of 1863**). Camp Banks, named for Captain Rolla Banks, Company D, 7th Minnesota Infantry Regiment, is located three miles north of Driscoll, Burleigh County.

Chaska's identity is as debated as his cause of death. There is some evidence that Chaska was also known as Wakinyatawa, or His Thunder, a ranking lieutenant of Little Crow, one of the principal leaders of the Dakota Conflict of 1862. Among the several hundred Indians tried and sentenced to hang after the conflict, several were named Chaska, and one was released because of testimony presented by George Spencer, a Minnesota fur trader.

Spencer told a harrowing tale of his capture during the conflict and his subsequent release due to Chaska, who rescued him at the risk of his own life. Later, Spencer was cared for by several Indian women, who were told to take him to Chaska's own home on the reservation. When Dakota raiding parties stopped Spencer and the women, the Dakota were told that Spencer was under the personal protection of Chaska. Spencer survived unharmed.

Was the Sibley scout named Chaska the same man who rescued George Spencer? It may never be known, but it is reported that the scout performed an act of heroism during the Sibley expedition. Chaska intervened on behalf of Lieutenant Ambrose Freeman and George Brackett when they were attacked while hunting antelope on the day of the Battle of Big Mound (see **Camp Whitney**).

The day Chaska died, Sibley's command started their homeward march around 5:00 a.m. They were headed northeast on a course parallel to their previous trail to the Missouri River. The men suffered from the heat and dehydration as they marched through land that was "hilly and stoney [sic]" and "bare as a closely cropped common."[15] Eventually, the column stopped at a lake for water and discovered an ancient Indian camp, which was possibly Menoken Indian Village State Historic Site.

After marching about twenty miles, the command "camped on the south side of a long, reedy bog hole" with knee-deep mud.[16] During the night, cannons and rockets were fired in hopes of attracting General Sully's attention. The effort was in vain; Sully and his men had been delayed at Fort Pierre and would not arrive in the area until the end of the month.

About 10:00 p.m. that night, Lieutenant L. W. Collins was told that Chaska was having a "fit." The lieutenant ran to Chaska's campsite and found him in a spasm. Collins dashed to the nearby dispensary for medicine, where he discovered the hospital steward in similar distress, although not as severe. Collins quickly prepared an emetic for both men and gave one to the steward. By the time he reached Chaska, the scout was dead.

When the steward recovered, he said that Chaska had come to the dispensary at about 9:00 p.m. seeking liniment to relieve back pain. The steward said that he and Chaska shared a small, residual quantity of alcohol that the steward had been transferring to another bottle. Examination of the original alcohol bottle revealed strychnine. It was thought that the bottle may have previously stored poison and that it was not properly washed before being filled with alcohol. Rumors abounded about Chaska's death. Some reports attribute his death to apoplexy (stroke), others suggest accidental poisoning, and some allege foul play. This historic mystery may never be solved.

More than a century later, the historic site preserves Camp Banks. There are several rifle pits on twenty acres of state land at the former military bivouac, although none of the pits are currently visible. A windbreak, two pole barns, and a small steel granary stand on the property, remnants of a former farmstead.

🪶 Double Ditch Indian Village

Double Ditch Indian Village State Historic Site, overlooking the Missouri River from its east banks, seven and one-half miles north of Bismarck, was once a large earthlodge village inhabited by Mandan Indians between A.D. 1600 and 1781. The remains of earthlodges and refuse mounds up to ten feet high are enclosed by two concentric fortification ditches (dry moats) that probably were surmounted by log palisades. The unique paired ditches set this village apart from others of the same time period.

According to Mandan oral history, their people lived in seven to nine villages near the mouth of the Heart River prior to Euro-American contact. The Mandans developed a rich and elaborate culture based on gardening and bison hunting. They raised corn, beans, squash, pumpkins, sunflowers, and tobacco on the river bottoms below their summer villages. These villages were centers of trade among themselves, nomadic Indian neighbors, and Euro-American traders.

The Mandans built dome-shaped houses of logs and earth which, when collapsed, appear as circular depressions. Earthlodge depressions average forty feet in diameter. The largest depression, probably the ruins of the ceremonial lodge, is near the center of the site adjacent to an open plaza area. Unlike older rectangular earthlodge villages where all of the front doors faced the same direction (see **Huff Indian Village**), the entrances to circular lodges faced in toward this central plaza.

The compact, fortified settlements of the time period indicate that these horticultural villages were threatened. As the name implies, two fortification ditches can be observed at Double Ditch, dug for defensive purposes. On the interior of each ditch there was a palisade line consisting of wooden poles that provided additional security. The exterior ditch is partially filled in the northwestern part of the site. The partial filling of this outer ditch supports the idea that the village contracted in size from a larger to smaller one through time. Archeologists believe that the original village was protected by a nine-foot deep, twenty-foot wide exterior ditch, and that after a smallpox epidemic, the settlement shrank in size, requiring a smaller fortification. There are approximately 56 house depressions enclosed in the inner moat and an additional 102 house depressions within the outer moat. The 1781 smallpox epidemic appears to have been responsible for the final abandonment of the site. In 1804 Lewis and Clark observed a band of Teton Dakota camping near the abandoned Mandan village. American Indian informants told them that the village had been vacant for about twenty-five years.

A Harvard University research group excavated a small part of the site in 1905. They investigated several middens (garbage heaps), a complex of storage pits, portions of lodge floors, and parts of the outer fortification ditch. No further excavation occurred at the site until the summer of 2002 when field work revealed the presence of two additional fortification trenches located beyond the previously known ditches. Additional research may substantially add to our understanding of this site. The site was acquired by the State Historical Society of North Dakota in 1936 and is listed on the National Register of Historic Places. Interpretive signs throughout the site provide a walking tour of the village.

Karl Bodmer's view of life in a Mandan chief's earthlodge home. Courtesy of Joslyn Art Museum.

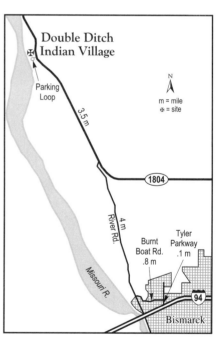

From: I-94 exit 157 at Bismarck, Burleigh County (L-12):
☞ North .1 mile on Tyler Parkway to Burnt Boat Drive ☞ West .8 mile on Burnt Boat Drive to River Road ☞ North 4 miles on River Road to ND•1804 ☞ North 3.5 miles to site access road on the west side of ND•1804 ☞ The .1 mile access road ends in a turnaround and the site is atop a hill north of the turnaround.

For a list of state and national historic sites, museums, and parks nearby, see page 155.

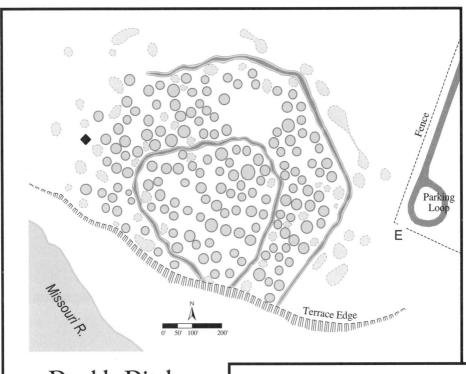

Double Ditch
Indian Village

E Entrance

◆ Information shelter (CCC)

⬤ Earthlodge depressions

☁ Midden mounds (refuse)

〰 Fortification ditch

Missouri R.

N

0' 50' 100'   200'

Terrace Edge

Fence

Parking Loop

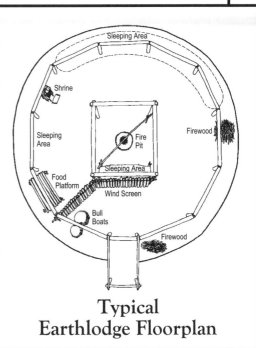

Typical
Earthlodge Floorplan

Sleeping Area

Shrine

Sleeping Area

Fire Pit

Firewood

Food Platform

Sleeping Area

Wind Screen

Bull Boats

Firewood

🏛 Former Governors' Mansion

The Former Governors' Mansion State Historic Site, located at 320 Avenue B in one of Bismarck's earliest residential areas, commemorates the North Dakota governors who resided there from 1893 to 1960. Constructed in 1884 by Bismarck businessman, Asa O. Fisher, the mansion was purchased by the State of North Dakota in 1893 for the sum of $5,000. The third governor of the state, Eli C. D. Shortridge, and his family moved in later that year.

Twenty-one chief executives subsequently occupied the mansion, with each family bringing their own changes in its decoration and, in some cases, its structure. The mansion was the site of social gatherings and state functions, and was the official home of the governor during a time in which the city of Bismarck changed dramatically. The mansion was one of the first houses in the city to have indoor plumbing, using a system that was obsolete by the 1930s. The carriage house from "horse-and-buggy" days was later converted into a garage. As the mansion became more and more antiquated, funds for construction of a new residence were finally approved by the 1955 Legislature. The last governor to occupy the mansion was John E. Davis, who moved to a new ranch-style governor's residence on the capitol grounds in 1960.

After its abandonment as the chief executive's home, the mansion housed the State Health Department from 1961 until 1975, when the house was transferred to the State Historical Society. Restoration work returned the building's exterior to its 1893 stick-style Victorian appearance. It is now an architectural and historic landmark in Bismarck and is listed on the National Register of Historic Places.

Governor Fred G. Aandahl, North Dakota's governor from 1948 to 1950, entertains his granddaughter in the north parlor at Christmas. SHSND C1858-03

Restoration of the building's interior focuses on preservation and the evolution of interior decor in this historic house. This unique approach has allowed original furniture and objects from different administrations to be placed together within the building, reflecting the mansion's continuous history. Interior walls, ceilings, and floors have exposed areas showing the many layers of paint and wallpaper used in the house over the years. Intensive research and documentation has helped to provide an understanding of the way the house was decorated during various periods, ensuring accuracy in placement of objects.

The Former Governors' Mansion is open May 16 through September 15 and is staffed by State Historical Society of North Dakota volunteers. Video programs of the mansion's history and restoration are featured. Admission is free, and donations are accepted. Partial funding for the mansion's restoration and maintenance is provided by the Society for Preservation of the Former Governors' Mansion. For more information and specific hours, contact the State Historical Society of North Dakota at (701) 328-2666.

At: Bismarck, Burleigh County (L-12):
☞ 320 East Avenue B

For a list of state and national historic sites, museums, and parks nearby, see page 155.

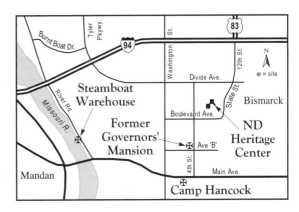

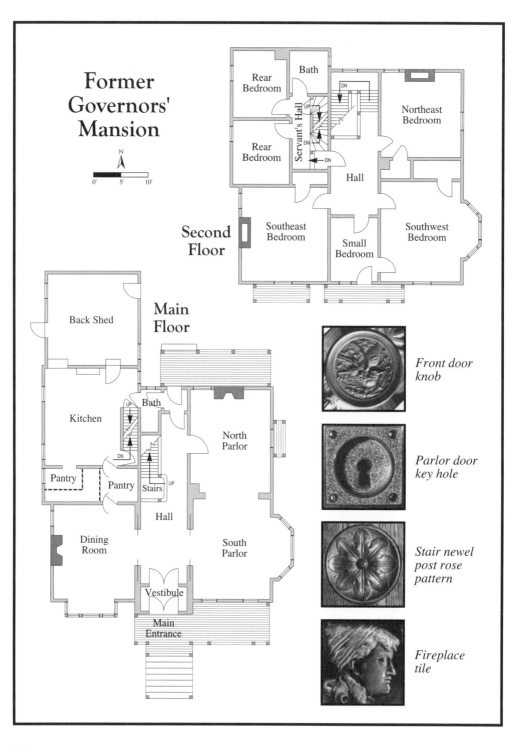

Former Governors' Mansion

N

0'   5'   10'

Second Floor

Rear Bedroom

Rear Bedroom

Bath

Servant's Hall

Northeast Bedroom

Hall

Southeast Bedroom

Small Bedroom

Southwest Bedroom

UP

DN

DN

DN

Main Floor

Back Shed

Kitchen

Bath

North Parlor

Pantry

Pantry

Stairs

Hall

Dining Room

South Parlor

Vestibule

Main Entrance

UP

DN

UP

Front door knob

Parlor door key hole

Stair newel post rose pattern

Fireplace tile

♠ Fort Ransom

Fort Ransom, established in 1867 to protect overland travel from Minnesota to Montana, was named in honor of brevet Major General Thomas E. G. Ransom of the U. S. Volunteers. Today, although the building locations and the dry moat are still clearly discernible, nothing else remains of the original fort or its twelve-foot high sod and log stockade. The historic site is located southwest of the town of Fort Ransom, Ransom County.

On June 17, 1867, a battalion of the 10th U.S. Infantry, commanded by brevet Major George H. Crosman, arrived from Fort Wadsworth. Soldiers began work on enclosing a breastwork and completed it by August. Oak logs from the nearby Sheyenne River Valley were used to construct the post. The buildings were arranged within the earthen breastworks in a square, measuring 350 by 400 feet. Ten square miles around the fort were designated as Fort Ransom Military Reservation, Dakota Territory.

With the exception of two, all were one-story log buildings. The barracks building was under one roof on the north side of the square and was subdivided into four large rooms for the enlisted men and two small rooms for the first sergeants. Box stoves warmed quarters, and each squad room had three windows. Kitchens were attached to the rear of the quarters. Other buildings at the post were quartermaster and commissary storehouses, quarters for married men, a granary, bakery, guardhouse, hospital, office for commandant and adjutant, stables, and the magazine. Outside the breastworks were quarters for the Indian scouts.

Survival at this military post, like any frontier settlement, was a constant struggle. Water for drinking and cooking had to be hauled from a spring 600 yards away. Facilities for bathing at the post were limited, and the nearby river was used for that purpose during the summer. The vegetable garden, eight acres in size, was near the post, and hay for livestock was harvested three miles to the south.

Quartermaster teams linked Fort Abercrombie to Fort Ransom, and a tri-weekly coach ran to St. Cloud, Minnesota. In winter the route from Fort Ransom to Fort Abercrombie was particularly dangerous due to storms, and in spring, flooding on the Wild Rice River stopped communication. In good weather the weekly mail by horseback via Fort Abercrombie took eight days to reach St. Paul, Minnesota.

Fort Ransom was dismantled in 1872, and the materials were used to build Fort Seward at Jamestown, Stutsman County. The army had determined that protection of the Northern Pacific Railroad crew at the James River crossing was a higher priority than protecting the overland route. The final disposition of the military reservation took place on July 14, 1880, when it was turned over to the Department of the Interior for survey and sale to homesteaders.

Today a marker describing the military fort sits beside a parking area on the east side of a county road. Building remnants and cellars, a fortification ditch with an embankment, and a flagpole mark the remains of this once thriving post.

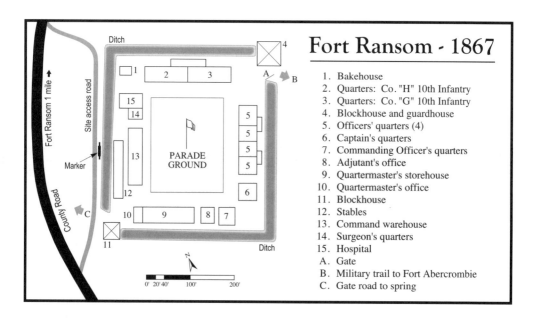

Fort Ransom - 1867

1. Bakehouse
2. Quarters: Co. "H" 10th Infantry
3. Quarters: Co. "G" 10th Infantry
4. Blockhouse and guardhouse
5. Officers' quarters (4)
6. Captain's quarters
7. Commanding Officer's quarters
8. Adjutant's office
9. Quartermaster's storehouse
10. Quartermaster's office
11. Blockhouse
12. Stables
13. Command warehouse
14. Surgeon's quarters
15. Hospital
A. Gate
B. Military trail to Fort Abercrombie
C. Gate road to spring

From: Fort Ransom, Ransom County (M-20):
☞ West and south .6 mile on asphalt road ☞ The site is east of the road.

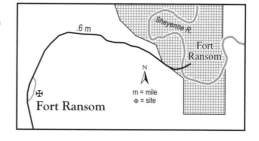

For a list of state and national historic sites, museums, and parks nearby, see page 156.

✠ Hudson Townsite

The Hudson Townsite State Historic Site, southwest of Oakes, Dickey County, marks the location of one of many speculative townsites established during the Great Dakota Boom (1879-1886) by people who hoped they could attract one or more railroads. This townsite is an example of the boom-bust settlement typical of the time. The plan to establish a town called Hudson began in 1883 with the formation of the Dakota Midland Railroad. A group of promoters headed by W. H. Becker met in Ellendale, Dakota Territory, where they organized the railroad, obtained a charter, secured right-of-way, and projected several townsites, including Hudson. The neophyte railroad would extend from Ellendale through Hudson to Wahpeton.

The townsite plat for Hudson was printed and widely circulated by M. N. Chamberlain, one of the promoters, who quickly settled down in the new town to sell land. The original town plat shows thirty blocks divided into twenty-five and fifty-foot lots, a central town square, where prospective buyers might envision a magnificent city hall, and extensive railroad depot grounds at the north end of town. The James River, with a projected ferry crossing, ran along the eastern edge of town.

The 1884 *Andreas Historical Atlas* lists two hotels, three stores, three real estate and loan offices, a printing office, newspaper, livery stable, pump shop, blacksmith shop, and post office in the fledgling town. The newspaper, the *Hudson Herald*, was established on December 14, 1883, by R. S. Busteed. A combination school and church building was erected in 1885.

During the spring and summer of 1886, enthusiasm for the townsite died when the Chicago and Northwestern Railroad pushed north to Oakes and laid its tracks on the east side of the James River opposite Hudson. That same year, the Northern Pacific Railway ran a branch line to Oakes. The next year the Sault Ste. Marie Railway acquired portions of the Dakota Midland's grade and pushed west into Oakes, thereby bypassing Hudson.

As soon as the ice froze on the James in the winter of 1886-1887, the town of Hudson was picked up and moved to Oakes. Buildings were placed on skids and dragged by horses and oxen across the ice. The few buildings remaining in Hudson were torn down for lumber or left to disintegrate. In less than three years, a town was born, boomed, and vanished. All that remains are faint depressions, piles of stones, and a few artifacts. The Hudson townsite was acquired by the State Historical Society in 1936. The marker was dedicated July 15, 1956.

The Hudson townsite is also near the July 17, 1839, camp site of the John C. Frémont and Joseph Nicolas Nicollet expedition, early geographers who explored water courses in the Northwest.

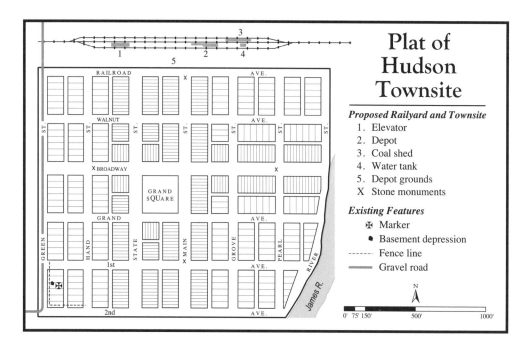

Plat of Hudson Townsite

Proposed Railyard and Townsite
1. Elevator
2. Depot
3. Coal shed
4. Water tank
5. Depot grounds
X Stone monuments

Existing Features
✠ Marker
• Basement depression
------ Fence line
—— Gravel road

From: Oakes, Dickey County (O-20):
☞ West 2 miles on asphalt road ☞ South 2.75 miles on gravel road
☞ The site is marked by an aluminum plaque on a fieldstone marker east of the road.

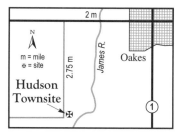

For a list of state and national historic sites, museums, and parks nearby, see page 156.

✠ Lake Jessie

Located west of the town of Jessie, Griggs County, Lake Jessie State Historic Site marks one of the camps of the Nicollet-Frémont expedition of 1839. Joseph Nicolas Nicollet, a French astronomer and cartographer, came to the United States to study the physical geography of North America. He wanted to explore the region between the Mississippi and Missouri rivers in the area that now makes up the states of Minnesota, North Dakota, and South Dakota. He was assisted by John Charles Frémont, a lieutenant in the Topographical Bureau of the Corps of Engineers. The lake was named for Jessie Ann Benton, daughter of Senator Thomas Hart Benton of Missouri. She later married John Frémont.

A campsite on the lake was also used by Isaac I. Stevens and his party on July 10-11, 1853, during a survey of a proposed railroad route. This was also a stopping point on July 15-16, 1862, July 20, 1863, and in 1866 by James L. Fisk and his wagon trains on their way to the Montana gold fields (see **Fort Dilts**). Mail carriers who crossed through the area between 1867 and 1872 sought shelter on the east end of Lake Jessie.

Enclosed by a fence, the site is .29 acres of state land, located on top of a hill beside a farmyard. An aluminum cast marker on a fieldstone and concrete monument describe the events that took place there. A flagpole stands north of the marker.

From: Binford, Griggs County (H-19):
☞ East 3.6 miles on ND•65 ☞ South .5 mile on gravel road ☞ West .75 mile Southwest .5 mile on dirt road past farmhouse ☞ The site is marked by an aluminum plaque on a fieldstone marker south of Lake Jessie.

For a list of state and national historic sites, museums, and parks nearby, see page 156.

↟ Lake Johnson

Lake Johnson State Historic Site is named for Private George T. Johnson (a.k.a. Johnston), who drowned in the lake on August 11, 1865. Soldiers from the 3rd Illinois Cavalry Regiment, who were camping nearby, were enjoying a refreshing swim on a hot August day when Private Johnson accidently drowned. He was buried near the campsite, and a headstone and flagpole currently stand there in his memory. The site is located seven miles southwest of Cooperstown, Griggs County.

The 3rd Illinois Cavalry Regiment, commanded by Colonel Robert Huston Carnahan, was en route from Fort Abercrombie to Devils Lake. The regiment was assisting the 1865 reconnaissance expedition of General Alfred Sully, which was exploring the territory between Fort Rice and Devils Lake. The information gathered by the mission was used ultimately to select the location of Fort Totten (see **Fort Totten**).

This is not the only historically significant event that transpired near Lake Johnson. The Nicollet-Frémont expedition in 1839 and the Isaac I. Stevens expedition in 1855 passed through this area (see **Lake Jessie**). On July 15, 1862, Captain James L. Fisk's wagon train of immigrants, who were traveling to the Montana gold fields, camped near the south end of this lake (see **Fort Dilts**). A year later on July 17, General Henry H. Sibley's military expedition crossed nearby heading toward Devils Lake (see **Sibley and Sully Expeditions of 1863**).

During the late 1860s and 1870s, military and post roads connecting Fort Abercrombie, Fort Ransom, and Fort Totten ran within a half mile of this site. The trail junction lies about three miles to the south and slightly to the west.

Forts
Abercrombie,
Ransom, &
Totten
Military Trail

♦ Fort
----- Military trail

Devils Lake

Ft. Totten

Lake Johnson

Valley City

Ft. Ransom

Ft. Abercrombie

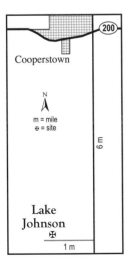

Cooperstown

200

N

m = mile
✠ = site

6 m

Lake
Johnson
✠

1 m

From: Cooperstown, Griggs County (I-20):
☞ South 6 miles from southeast edge of Cooperstown on asphalt road ☞ West 1 mile on gravel road ☞ The site is marked by a white headstone and a flagpole north of the road.

For a list of state and national historic sites, museums, and parks nearby, see page 156.

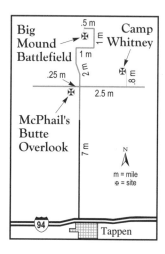

From: Tappen, Kidder County (K-15):
☞ North 7 miles on asphalt/gravel road
☞ West .25 mile on gravel road ☞ The site is marked by a pink granite marker atop a hill to the southwest.

↟ McPhail's Butte Overlook

McPhail's Butte Overlook State Historic Site marks one place from which Colonel Samuel McPhail directed movements of the 1st Minnesota Mounted Rangers during the Battle of Big Mound, July 24, 1863. This was the first battle that the Sibley expedition fought against Dakota Indians (see **Sibley and Sully Expeditions of 1863**). The site is located seven and one-half miles north of Tappen, Kidder County.

Following the tragic opening of the battle (see **Big Mound Battlefield**), Colonel McPhail's cavalry prevented the Indians from escaping over the western edge of the plateau where they had been driven. Taking a position on the highest point at the western edge of the plateau, McPhail saw Indians moving south off the plateau through ravines opening onto the plains below. As the troopers pursued, a bolt of lightning struck, killing Private John Murphy and knocking two other soldiers to the ground.

Undeterred, McPhail's troops pursued the Indians for fourteen miles from the plateau to Dead Buffalo Lake, one mile north of the present-day town of Dawson. As darkness fell, the soldiers began setting up a temporary camp, but soon received orders to return to the main camp. The troops marched most of the night to return to Camp Sibley, gathering other regiments already encamped on the marshy plain. In all they had covered nearly fifty miles and fought a major battle with no food and little water.

A granite marker erected on top of a high hill denotes Colonel McPhail's vantage point overlooking the battle. There is, however, no access road, and a barbed wire fence separates the historic site from the county road. For access information, contact the Historic Preservation Division, State Historical Society of North Dakota, 612 East Boulevard Avenue, Bismarck, North Dakota, 58505, or call (701) 328-2666.

For a list of state and national historic sites, museums, and parks nearby, see page 156.

⚒ Menoken Indian Village

Menoken Indian Village State Historic Site is located near the town of Menoken, east of Bismarck. Once thought to be the "Mantanne Fort" (Mandan village) visited by the 1738 La Vérendrye expedition, recent studies show it to be one of the earliest Plains Village sites in the state, predating the La Vérendrye expedition by hundreds of years.

How did this case of mistaken identity happen? The letters written by the members of the La Vérendrye family are the earliest records of Europeans traveling on the northern plains. These documents contain clues to the location of the village visited by the expedition. Traveling with Assiniboin guides, Pierre Gaultier de Varennes, the Sieur de la Vérendrye, and his sons left the confluence of the Red and Assiniboine Rivers (in modern-day Manitoba) and entered the area that would become North Dakota. Because they did not know the names of the landmarks they passed, the record of their journey is unclear. While in the area, the expedition stayed at a fortified Mandan village of approximately 130 lodges located several miles from the Missouri River. They also noted many cache (storage) pits in the village.

The actual location of the village visited by the La Vérendrye expedition is still under debate, but two of the state's earliest archeologists, George Will and Thaddeus C. Hecker, believed that Menoken village was the place. Hecker, under the direction of Will, conducted archeological excavations at the site in 1938 and 1939 using Works Progress Administration funds. Hecker dug one complete lodge, parts of four other lodges, and one bastion. He found that the lodges were oval rather than round in shape and were built in a depression. Hecker discovered that, unlike typical earthlodge construction, these lodges had none of the underground cache pits for storing food described by La Vérendrye. Also, there was relatively little pottery or bone tools. The only European trade goods contemporary with the La Vérendrye expedition were found outside the ditch.

Lacking modern dating techniques, such as radiocarbon, Hecker and Will concluded that the site was a Late Mandan village occupied after A.D. 1750. Their primary piece of evidence was that, of the earthlodge villages they knew, the Menoken village was one of the few not beside the Missouri River. Because of its unique location on Apple Creek some distance from the Missouri River, they believed that it was the Mandan village visited by the 1738 La Vérendrye expedition. Based upon their research, Menoken was designated a National Historic Landmark on July 19, 1964.

Since then archeologists have learned that earthlodge villages have been found along many of the major streams in the state, such as the James, Sheyenne, and Little Missouri rivers. Later research determined the Menoken village is too small to have held the 130 lodges described by La Vérendrye. The site covers 2.5 acres and has about twenty lodges. These homes are difficult to see, but several appear as faint, shallow depressions outlined by darker vegetation. The ruins of the earth homes are enclosed by a fortification ditch with four bastions (projecting curves in the dry moat). A few additional lodges may be located outside the ditch.

Archeologists now believe that Menoken Indian Village State Historic Site existed much before the La Vérendrye expedition. This classification is based on the way the lodges were constructed and on the types of artifacts that are found there. The village was occupied around A.D. 1200 based on radiocarbon dating of seeds recovered during archeological excavations in 1998 and 1999. Further archeological research at the site is needed to determine its age and identify the inhabitants of this significant village.

A fieldstone kiosk at the entrance to the historic site contains a map and brief interpretive information. Additional interpretive signs are located in the village site.

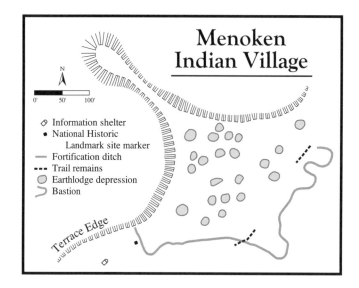

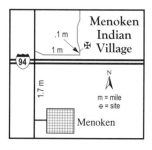

From: Menoken,
Burleigh County (L-12):
☞ West .3 mile to asphalt road
☞ North 1.7 miles to gravel frontage road on north side of I-94
☞ East 1 mile on gravel road
☞ North .1 mile ☞ Northeast .1 mile on dirt road ☞ The site is marked by a fieldstone kiosk.

For a list of state and national historic sites, museums, and parks nearby, see page 157.

98

🏛 North Dakota Heritage Center

The North Dakota Heritage Center, located on the state capitol grounds off Exit 159 on I-94 in Bismarck, is the headquarters of the State Historical Society of North Dakota and the largest museum in the state. Opened in 1981, it features temporary and permanent exhibits that explore the story of life on the northern plains from prehistory to the present. In the main gallery, the "Corridor of Time" exhibit presently under development covers more than 100 million years of history in North Dakota and features fossils of ancient creatures such as the champsosaurus and the mosasaur (above, right). Other exhibits highlight native cultures from the time of the glaciers 10,000 years ago to the first contacts with Euro-Americans. Exhibits on the fur trade era, including the story of the Lewis and Clark expedition, tell of economic competition and military conflict over a vast prairie empire. More stories document the struggles and successes of the homesteaders and pioneers, the economic "boom" of the early twentieth century, and the disillusioning "bust" of the 1930s. Visitors can experience history through hundreds of objects, view images of the past through photographs and actual films made from 1916 to 1921, and participate in interactive exhibits such as cranking a Model-T or even smelling a buffalo wallow. The magnificent silver service of the U.S.S. *North Dakota* is an example of the exhibits to be found in the special galleries of the Heritage Center.

Welcoming more than 100,000 visitors annually, the Heritage Center is the only museum in the state accredited by the American Association of Museums. It houses extensive artifact, archeological, photographic, and archival collections. In a cooperative agreement with the North Dakota Geological Survey, the Heritage Center also houses the State Fossil Collection.

The State Archives and Historical Research Library, located at the Heritage Center, is responsible for the documentary collections of the State Historical Society of North Dakota. It is the official state archive, and acquires and preserves all types of research materials relating to North Dakota and the northern great plains, including manuscript collections, books, periodicals, maps, newspapers, audio and video materials, and photographs. It is open to the public and is particularly valuable to individuals doing genealogical research.

The North Dakota Heritage Center is open weekdays from 8 a.m. to 5 p.m., Saturdays from 9 a.m. to 5 p.m., and Sundays from 11 a.m. to 5 p.m. Admission is free. The State Archives and Historical Research Library is open 8 a.m. to 4:30 p.m., Monday through Friday, and the State Historical Society of North Dakota offices are open 8 a.m. to 5 p.m., Monday through Friday, except holidays. For more information, call (701) 328-2666, or visit the Society's web site at http://www. DiscoverND.com/hist.

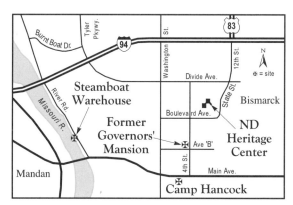

At: Bismarck, Burleigh County (L-12):
612 East Boulevard Avenue, North Dakota Capitol Grounds.

For a list of state and national historic sites, museums, and parks nearby, see page 157.

🦅 Standing Rock

Perched on a high hill overlooking the Sheyenne River in Ransom County are a series of four interconnected burial mounds. Three of the mounds are circular, artificial hills in the shape of low cones. The fourth is a linear mound, which extends in a straight line. It begins west of the central mounds and runs east to the farthest conical mound (see map). The site is named after a large boulder that stands on the top of the largest mound.

Burial mounds are human cemeteries that contain multiple graves and were built primarily during the middle of the Woodland period, dating from 100 B.C. to A.D. 600 (see **Pulver Mounds**). Some mounds continued to be used as a place of interment for more than a thousand years. A single conical mound can contain up to thirty-five individuals.

Travelers used the Standing Rock mounds as a landmark. The 1843 map prepared by Joseph Nicollet identifies "Inyan Bosndata or Standing Rock" (see map). According to linguist Dr. Robert Hollow, the correct spelling should be *Íyá Bósdata*, which means "Standing Rock" in Santee Sioux. Nicollet and John C. Frémont camped within sight of the site on Monday, August 12, 1839 (see **Lake Jessie** for more information about the Nicollet and Frémont expedition). From March 1881 to July 1884, the local post office was called "Standingrock," because the Post Office Department refused to accept post office names of more than one word.

The site is two miles east of Little Yellowstone Park, near Enderlin, Ransom County. The access road to the site climbs a steep hill and access depends on weather and road conditions. There is a gravel parking lot at the top of the hill. A monument beside the mounds gives a brief description of the significance of this prehistoric cemetery.

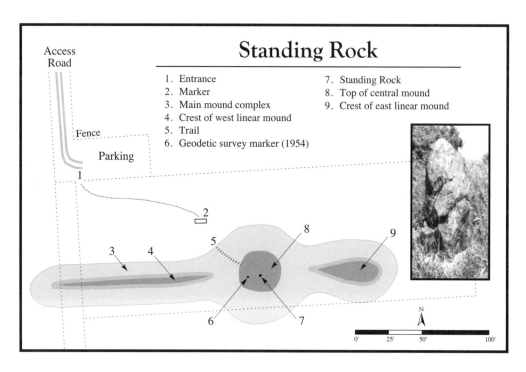

Standing Rock

Access
Road

1. Entrance
2. Marker
3. Main mound complex
4. Crest of west linear mound
5. Trail
6. Geodetic survey marker (1954)
7. Standing Rock
8. Top of central mound
9. Crest of east linear mound

Fence

Parking

N

0'   25'   50'   100'

Nicollet & Frémont
1839 Trail

Devils Lake

Lake
Jessie

Standing
Rock

Valley
City

Jamestown

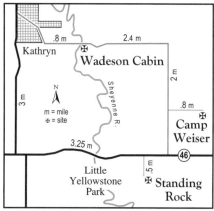

.8 m   2.4 m

Kathryn   Wadeson Cabin

2 m

Sheyenne R.

3 m

N
m = mile
⊕ = site

.8 m

Camp
Weiser

3.25 m

Little
Yellowstone
Park

.5 m

46

Standing
Rock

From: Kathryn, Barnes County (L-20):
☞ South 3 miles on asphalt road to ND•46 ☞ East 3.25 miles on ND•46 ☞ South .5 mile on dirt road up a steep hill ☞ The site is marked by three mounds, a large cylindrical stone, and an aluminum plaque on a fieldstone marker.

For a list of state and national historic sites, museums, and parks nearby, see page 157.

ᛈ Steamboat Warehouse

The Steamboat Warehouse Historic Marker, located on the east bank of the Missouri River in Bismarck across the road from the water treatment plant on River Road (Highway 1804), commemorates the Northern Pacific Railroad warehouse built to store goods in transshipment between steamboats and freight trains. The 300-foot-long stone and frame warehouse was constructed in 1883 and was torn down in 1925. The interpretive marker also describes activity at the dock adjacent to the warehouse.

From 1872 to 1887 Bismarck was an important transportation center and Missouri River port. Freight was hauled to Bismarck from the East by the Northern Pacific Railroad. Until a railroad bridge across the Missouri was completed October 21, 1882, the railroad terminated at the east side of the river and resumed on the west side. During the winter, trains crossed the ice on specially built track and during the summer, they were ferried across. A line called the River Landing Spur ran down to the steamboat warehouse so that freight from the railroad could be transferred to steamboats for shipping via the Missouri River. The river connected St. Louis, Missouri, Fort Benton, Montana, and ports in between.

The dock area included other warehouses, saloons, hotels, restaurants, and gambling establishments built to service the transient river trade. Bismarck was a major distribution point and travel center during that time and continued to serve in a reduced manner even after the railroad continued west in 1883.

This 3.21 acre site displays a fieldstone monument with an aluminum plaque and is open year-round. A small parking area is in front of the marker on the west side of the road.

A steamboat, the freight house, and in the distance, the brewery in Bismarck, 1886. SHSND E0155

At: Bismarck, Burleigh County (L-12):
☞ North .1 mile on Tyler Parkway to Burnt Boat Drive ☞ West .8 mile on Burnt Boat Drive to River Road ☞ South 1.4 miles on River Road ☞ The site is marked by an aluminum plaque on a fieldstone marker west of the road.

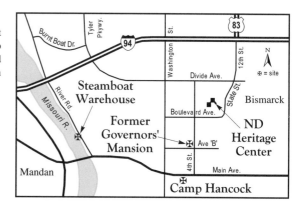

For a list of state and national historic sites, museums, and parks nearby, see page 157.

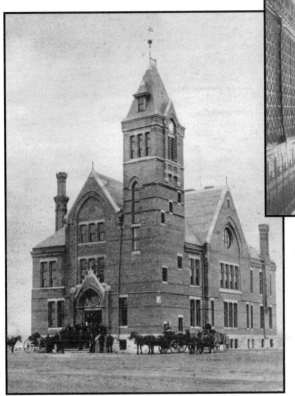

The Stutsman County Courthouse is pictured in an early photo (left, SHSND 1005-2). The interior contains many examples of pressed metal wall and ceiling coverings (above, SHSND AHP 32SN45-03).

🏛 Stutsman County Courthouse

Stutsman County Courthouse, located at 504 Third Avenue SE in Jamestown, is the oldest surviving courthouse in North Dakota and is listed on the National Register of Historic Places. During the days of the Dakota Territory, meetings were held in the courthouse in preparation for statehood. The building is considered a superb but rare example in the Upper Midwest of the Gothic-Revival style of architecture. The interior is outstanding for its stamped metal ornamentation that dates to 1905.

Designed by Henry C. Koch, a Wisconsin architect who worked as General Philip H. Sheridan's topographic engineer during the Civil War, the courthouse construction was completed in 1883. An addition designed by Gilbert R. Horton, a Jamestown architect, was added on the rear of the courthouse in 1926 to handle the growing needs of Stutsman County. The building served as the center of county government until the early 1980s when a new courthouse was built, adjoining and incorporating the earlier addition.

Restoration efforts have stabilized the exterior of the courthouse. Rehabilitation is dependent upon future availability of funds. To make a contribution to the restoration of this significant monument, contact the State Historical Society of North Dakota, 612 E. Boulevard Ave., Bismarck, North Dakota, 58205, or call (701) 328-2666.

The building's ornate rose window illuminates the courtroom's pressed metal ceiling. SHSND AHP 32SN45-03

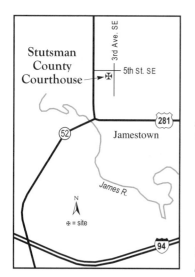

At: Jamestown, Stutsman County (K-18):
☞ 504 3rd Avenue, SE

For a list of state and national historic sites, museums, and parks nearby, see page 158.

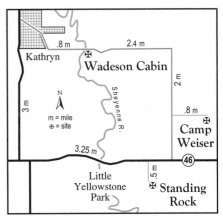

From: Kathryn, Barnes County (L-20):
☞ East .8 mile on gravel road across the Sheyenne River ☞ The site is marked by an aluminum plaque on a fieldstone marker and a cabin south of the road by the river.

⊞ Wadeson Cabin

A hand-hewn oak log cabin, with dovetailed corners, stands on its original fieldstone foundation at Wadeson Cabin State Historic Site. It was built in 1876 by Carl Jenson and his nephew Jon Bjerke on the east bank of the Sheyenne River near Kathryn, Barnes County. The cabin has served as a community hall, country store, pioneer home, and, finally, as an icehouse. A marker, beside a small parking area on the north side of the building, presents a short history of the site.

The original one and one-half story cabin contained a single, rectangular room on the main floor. Later, a lean-to was added to the north side, as indicated by a shadow mark (line on the exterior wall) on the gable end. The lean-to is missing. At one time portions of the building were covered with brick-patterned pressed metal, and later the gable ends were protected with tar paper. The only openings in the simple building are a door flanked by a window on the east side, a window on the south side of the main story, and one above in the gable end.

Archeological excavations conducted in 1980 and 1981 uncovered a flagstone threshold in the doorway. Little else was found due to the installation of a deep cellar when the building was used as an icehouse. The building was restored in 1981.

For a list of state and national historic sites, museums, and parks nearby, see page 158.

✦ Whitestone Hill Battlefield

Whitestone Hill Battlefield State Historic Site, located twenty-three miles southeast of Kulm, Dickey County, marks the scene of the fiercest clash between Indians and white soldiers in North Dakota. On September 3, 1863, General Alfred Sully's troops attacked a tipi camp of Yanktonai, some Dakota, Hunkpapa Lakota, and Blackfeet (Sihasapa Lakota), as part of a military mission to punish participants of the Dakota Conflict of 1862 (see **Sibley and Sully Expeditions of 1863**). In the ensuing battle, many Indian men, women, and children died or were captured. Military casualties were comparatively light. The Indians also suffered the destruction of virtually all of their property, leaving them nearly destitute for the coming winter.

That morning, Major Albert E. House, a Battalion Commander of the Sixth Iowa Cavalry, led a scouting party in search of Indians. In the early afternoon, their Métis guide, Frank LaFrambois, discovered a small encampment of Sioux on a small lake near Whitestone Hill. LaFrambois notified Major House, who moved his battalion toward the village. Upon closer reconnaissance, House discovered that the "small" encampment included 300 to 600 lodges. Frank LaFrambois and two soldiers were dispatched to notify General Sully of the discovery and to request reinforcements. While they were gone, the Indians detected the presence of the troops, and some of the villagers prepared to flee, while others prepared to fight. Major House sent two reconnaissance parties to opposite sides of the tipi encampment to gather tactical information while he waited for the main column to arrive. For nearly three hours, an uneasy stand-off continued during which a delegation of Indian elders approached the soldiers and offered to surrender some of their chiefs. House, however, insisted on total surrender, and negotiations broke down.

Sully's command was less than a mile away when the Indians saw them coming, and departure preparations became frantic. Tipis were stripped, travois were hastily attached to ponies and dogs, and possessions and small children were strapped to the travois. Masses of Indians began streaming east, down a ravine that opened into a shallow mouth at the rear of the village. It was nearly sunset when Sully's troops reached the scouting party.

As Sully's main column advanced toward the village, it became apparent that the Indians were escaping. Sully ordered Colonel Robert W. Furnas, commanding the Second Nebraska Cavalry, forward at full speed to cut off the Indians' retreat. Stopping briefly to instruct Major House to circle around to the left (north and east), Furnas directed his men around to the right (south), hoping to encircle the village. Seeing that Whitestone Hill blocked escape to the south, Sully sent Colonel David S. Wilson, with part of the Sixth Iowa, to the north side of the village.

General Sully, with one company of the Seventh Iowa Cavalry, two companies of the Sixth Iowa Cavalry, and the artillery battery, charged toward the center of the village. As they passed through the village, they captured a number of prisoners, who were left behind under guard. Sully and his troops climbed to the top of Whitestone Hill to direct the rest of the battle and to offer artillery support, if needed by the soldiers on the flats below.

Although the Indians scattered in as many directions as possible, most tried to escape down the ravine. As the Indians came to a saucer-like broadening of the ravine about one-half mile from the village, they began to gather in a large throng. There they were surrounded by Colonel Furnas's cavalry, Major House's battalion, and Colonel Wilson's Sixth Iowa troops.

Fearing that the Indians might escape in the impending darkness, Furnas ordered his men to dismount and advance toward the ravine on foot. When his men were within a few hundred yards, he ordered them to begin firing. The other troops followed his lead, dismounted, and closed in on the Indians. Only Wilson's men remained mounted, and, as the attack continued, their horses became wild and unmanageable. The Indians, noticing this weakness in the north firing line, suddenly charged in that direction. Many were able to escape the deadly ravine.

As darkness deepened, Colonel Furnas suspected that bullets from the other units were hitting his lines. He withdrew his troops to higher ground surrounding the ravine. As Furnas and his men withdrew, the other units also broke off the engagement and spent the night on the hilltops overlooking the battlefield.

The light of the following day revealed a field of carnage. Dead and wounded men, women, and children, lay in the campsite and in the ravine. Tipis stood vacant, or drooped in various stages of destruction. Camp equipment and personal items, tools, utensils, weapons, toys, and injured or dying horses and dogs littered the ground. Injured women protected babies and little children. As the soldiers looked after the wounded and gathered the dead, Sully moved his camp to the battlefield. While some squads of soldiers patrolled the region searching for escapees, other men were put to work digging graves and destroying the village and Indian possessions.

During the Battle of Whitestone Hill, 20 soldiers were killed and 38 were wounded. Although there was no accurate count of the Indian casualties, estimates ranged from 100 to 300 dead. In addition, 32 men and 124 women and children were captured. For two days, military patrols guarded against reprisal raids while troops destroyed Indian property. Tipis, buffalo hides, wagons, travois, blankets, and perhaps as much as a half million pounds of buffalo meat were stacked and burned. Some of the fires were set over the graves of the soldiers to obscure the location of the burial places. Troops threw pots, kettles, weapons, and other things that would sink into the lake.

On September 5, one of the scouting details ran into a party of Indians. In the ensuing skirmish, two more white soldiers were killed. The following day, Sully and his army marched south toward their transport on the Missouri River. The Indians, who had escaped the battlefield, scattered over the plains looking for friends and families who could share necessities during the winter months.

Today, Whitestone Battlefield State Historic Site includes a portion of the battlefield and a small museum with exhibits explaining the 1863 Sibley and Sully expeditions and the Battle of Whitestone Hill. There are two monuments, one honoring the Indian dead and a second commemorating the soldiers who died in the battle. A marker also recognizes two early settlers, Tom and Mary Shimmin. A fieldstone shelter beside the trail provides a resting point overlooking part of the battlefield and a freshwater lake. Nearby is a picnic area with a shelter, table, horseshoe pits, pit toilets, and a parking lot. The site is open May 16 through September 15, Thursday through Monday. Admission is free, and donations are accepted.

Brochures describing the site are available from the State Historical Society of North Dakota. For more information and specific hours, contact the Site Supervisor, Whitestone Hill Battlefield State Historic Site, R. R. 1, Box 125, Kulm, North Dakota, 58456, or call (701) 396-7731.

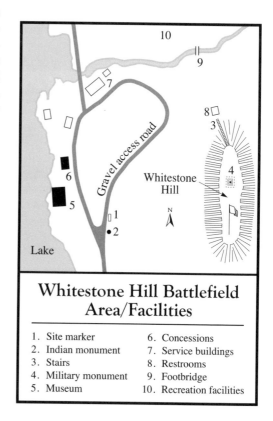

From: Kulm, LaMoure County (N-17):
☞ South 12 miles on ND•56 ☞ East 4 miles on gravel road ☞ North 1.75 miles to the site ☞ The site is marked by a small museum, cemetery, and monuments.

Whitestone Hill Battlefield Area/Facilities

1. Site marker	6. Concessions
2. Indian monument	7. Service buildings
3. Stairs	8. Restrooms
4. Military monument	9. Footbridge
5. Museum	10. Recreation facilities

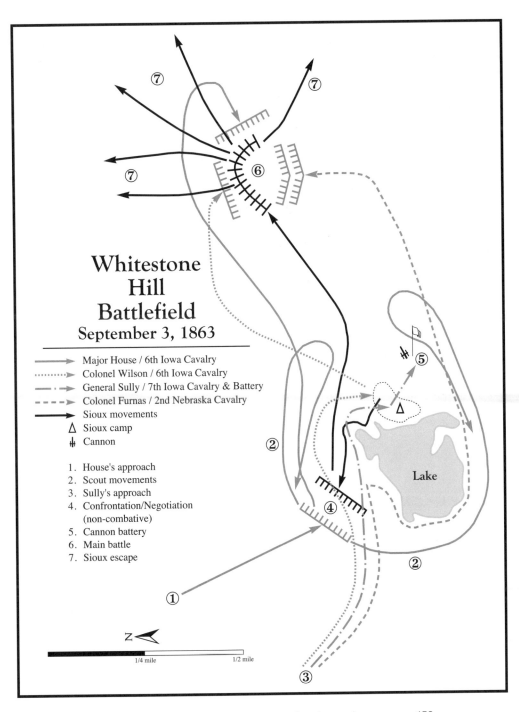

Whitestone Hill Battlefield
September 3, 1863

- → Major House / 6th Iowa Cavalry
- ⋯▸ Colonel Wilson / 6th Iowa Cavalry
- ·–·▸ General Sully / 7th Iowa Cavalry & Battery
- --→ Colonel Furnas / 2nd Nebraska Cavalry
- → Sioux movements
- △ Sioux camp
- ⚓ Cannon

1. House's approach
2. Scout movements
3. Sully's approach
4. Confrontation/Negotiation (non-combative)
5. Cannon battery
6. Main battle
7. Sioux escape

Lake

N

1/4 mile   1/2 mile

For a list of state and national historic sites, museums, and parks nearby, see page 158.

Lakes & Gardens

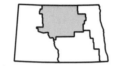

▲ *State Historical Society Sites*
△ *Other Sites*

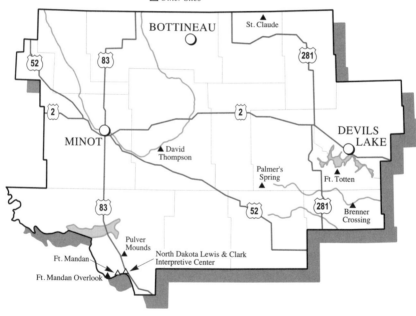

✠ Brenner Crossing

Brenner Crossing State Historic Site lies near the military trail linking Fort Totten, near Devils Lake, to Fort Seward, near Jamestown. The actual river crossing, named for Ernest Brenner (above, SHSND C1396), is located several miles away on the Sheyenne River. The site is northeast of New Rockford, Eddy County, but is unmarked and has no visible remnants of the trail or other archeological features.

Ernest William Brenner, born May 30, 1844, in Germany, came to the United States with his parents in 1848 and settled in Boston, Massachusetts. His varied career began as a page for two Massachusetts governors and later included scouting for General Banks and clerking for the adjutant general. In 1868 he became the post trader at Fort Totten. He remained at the fort until 1882, when he left and began farming on the south bank of the Sheyenne River along the Fort Totten-Fort Seward trail.

In addition to farming, Brenner ran a river crossing and established a post office, where he served as postmaster. His enterprise was not a financial success, and in April 1887, he was appointed to be government agent (farmer-in-chief) at the Turtle Mountain Indian Reservation. The Brenner post office was discontinued April 23, 1887.

Brenner and his wife Mary had a daughter, Christina, who married Alexander Charlebois. Brenner's wife was the daughter of Pierre Bottineau, scout and guide, for whom the city and county are named.

From: New Rockford, Eddy County (H-17):
☞ East 15 miles on ND•15 ☞ North 3 miles on gravel road
☞ East 1 mile ☞ North 2 miles ☞ West .1+ mile ☞ The site
is unmarked on the south side of the road.

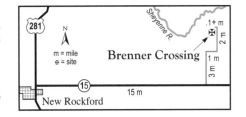

For a list of state and national historic sites, museums, and parks nearby, see page 158.

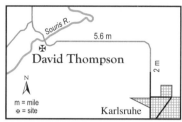

From: Karlsruhe, McHenry County (F-12):
☞ North 2 miles on asphalt/gravel road
☞ West 5.6 miles on gravel road ☞ The
site is marked by a granite globe south of
the road.

✠ David Thompson

David Thompson, explorer, fur trader, and the first European to explore the entire length of the Columbia River, was called by a contemporary "the greatest geographer of his day in British America." To honor his accomplishments as a geographer and astronomer, the David Thompson State Historic Site is marked by a granite globe atop a rectangular granite base, northeast of Velva, McHenry County.

David Thompson was born in Westminster, England, on April 30, 1770. He was educated at London's Grey Coat School, a charitable institution. When he was fourteen years old, he left school and became an apprentice to the Hudson's Bay Company to learn clerking, surveying, and hunting. In 1797, after finishing his apprenticeship, he joined the Northwest Company, a formidable fur trade competitor of his former employer.

As part of his first trading assignment, an attempt to establish a trading alliance with the Mandan and Hidatsa Indians living in a group of villages at the mouth of the Knife River (currently **Knife River Indian Villages National Historic Site**), Thompson was entrusted with the task of mapping the Northwest Company's posts and determining their relationship to the American border. Although the border was understood to run westward along the 49th parallel to the Rocky Mountains, it was still in dispute. Thompson passed near the historic site while on this assignment, leaving the Souris River a short distance west of the confluence of the Wintering River with the Souris on December 23, 1797. Thompson's surveys and observations from this expedition led to the first reliable map of the region from the west bend of the Souris River to the western shore of Lake Superior, a map used by Lewis and Clark during their expedition across North America.

Thompson continued his explorations and observations for another fifteen years, and the exploration of the Columbia River was his most famous accomplishment. In 1812 Thompson retired from active trading and exploration. He settled in Terrebonne, Quebec, where he finished his great map of the Northwest. For ten years Thompson worked for the International Boundary Commission, and during his last years, he completed the narrative of his experiences. He and his Scotch-Cree wife, Charlotte, raised thirteen children. David Thompson died February 10, 1857.

The David Thompson State Historic Site is enclosed by a barbed wire fence and overlooks the beautiful Souris River Valley. The Great Northern Railroad donated the land to the state and commissioned and erected the monument, which was dedicated on July 17, 1925. The pedestal under the globe bears the following inscription:

1770   DAVID THOMPSON   1857
Geographer and Astronomer

Passed near here in 1797 and 1798 on a scientific and trading expedition.
He made the first map of the country which is now North Dakota and
achieved many noteworthy discoveries in the Northwest.

A detail from a map drawn by David Thompson for the North West Company. Taken from The Manuscript Journals of Alexander Henry and of David Thompson, *Vol. III, Elliott Coues, editor (New York: Francis P. Harper, 1897). SHSND 971 H39 V.3*

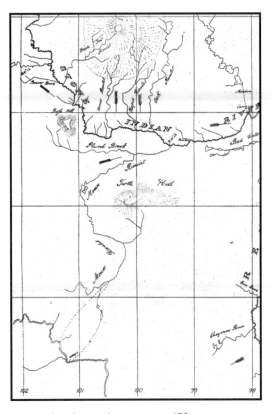

For a list of state and national historic sites, museums, and parks nearby, see page 159.

✠ Fort Mandan

This full-sized reconstruction of Fort Mandan, the home of the Lewis and Clark Expedition during the winter of 1804-05, stands along the Missouri River near Washburn, North Dakota. It is not certain how close this site is to the original Fort Mandan, which burned during the winter following the expedition's stay. Most scholars believe that the site of the original fort has been flooded by the Missouri River.

The reconstruction of the fort, completed twenty-five years ago, was based upon descriptions found in the journals of the expedition. Patrick Gass, a member of the expedition, described the fort as follows:

> [T]he huts were in two rows, containing four rooms each, and joined at one end forming an angle. When raised about 7 feet high a floor of puncheons or split plank were laid, and covered with grass and clay; which made a warm loft. The upper part projected a foot over and the roofs were made shed-fashion, rising from the inner side, and making the outer wall about 18 feet high. The part not inclosed by the huts we intended to picket. In the angle formed by the two rows of huts we built two rooms, for holding our provisions and stores.[17]

The fort was constructed of the cottonwood timber found along the Missouri. Construction began on November 3, 1804, and Gass records that by the evening of November 27, they had completed the roofs of their huts, which were made of "puncheon split out of cotton wood and then hewed." That night, seven inches of snow fell, and the following day was stormy.

A steady stream of Mandan and Hidatsa Indians visited during the five months the expedition spent at Fort Mandan, trading goods and information about the land to the west. Lewis and Clark and other members of the expedition also made frequent visits to the nearby villages and went on joint hunting trips with the villagers during that winter. On April 7, 1805, the expedition left Fort Mandan, on their way to the Pacific Ocean, after spending longer at this location than they would anywhere else on their journey.

The reconstructed Fort Mandan is equipped with replica furnishings, and interpreters in period attire are on-site daily. The site contains a visitor service center and picnic areas. It is located on McLean County Highway 17, two miles north of the North Dakota Lewis and Clark Interpretive Center at Washburn. Fort Mandan is open from 9 a.m. to 7 p.m., Memorial Day through Labor Day and from 9 a.m. to 5 p.m. the rest of the year. There is an admission fee that covers both Fort Mandan and the Interpretive Center. For more information contact North Dakota Lewis and Clark Interpretive Center, P.O. Box 607, Washburn, ND 58577-0607, call (701) 462-8535 or toll-free (877) 462-8535, fax: (701) 462-3316, e-mail info@fortmandan.org, or visit the web site at www.fortmandan.com.

In 1807 Sergeant Patrick Gass, a member of the Corps of Discovery, published his own journal of the expedition. Included in the journal was this illustration of expedition members building Fort Mandan in the late fall of 1804. SHSND C572

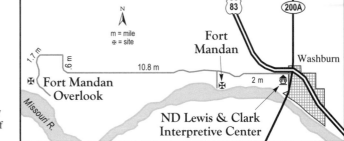

From: Washburn, McLean County (I-11):
☞ West 2 miles on McLean County Highway 17 from the intersection of US•83 and ND•200A.

Fort Mandan - Overhead View

- from a journal map drawn by William Clark

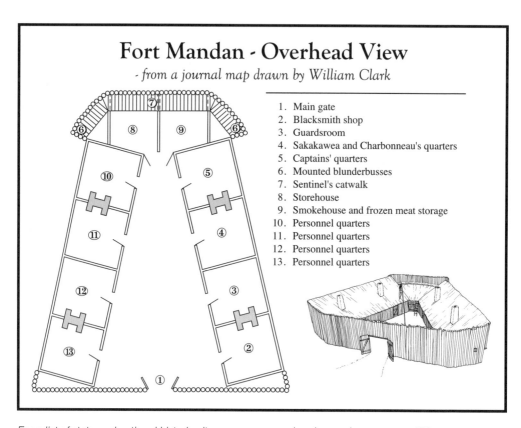

1. Main gate
2. Blacksmith shop
3. Guardsroom
4. Sakakawea and Charbonneau's quarters
5. Captains' quarters
6. Mounted blunderbusses
7. Sentinel's catwalk
8. Storehouse
9. Smokehouse and frozen meat storage
10. Personnel quarters
11. Personnel quarters
12. Personnel quarters
13. Personnel quarters

For a list of state and national historic sites, museums, and parks nearby, see page 159.

✠ Fort Mandan Overlook

Fort Mandan Overlook is so named because the site overlooks the area where Lewis and Clark established their headquarters, called Fort Mandan, in the winter of 1804-1805. Fort Mandan was a triangular fort which provided shelter, protection, and a place of cultural interchange between the explorers and the area's Indian inhabitants, for whom the fort was named. The original site of Fort Mandan was beside the river and has been inundated.

In 1991-1992 State Historical Society archeologists excavated part of the site, which lies fourteen miles west of Washburn, McLean County, overlooking the Missouri River. Based on these studies, we now know that people lived at this location during two different times: once during the late-1700s to mid-1800s and earlier, around A.D. 1300 to 1400. An irregular ditch constructed sometime during the late-eighteenth century to mid-nineteenth century is the most visible feature at this archeological site. At present no historic documents have been found that identify the date of construction of the ditch, the builders, or the events that transpired there. Historic-period artifacts found in the sod and just below it include glass trade beads, a gunflint, lead shot, and glass fragments.

Although the historic events at the site remain a puzzle, the prehistoric use is better understood. A significant Plains Village campsite was discovered by the archeologists. While no houses were detected during excavation or are visible on the ground surface, contemporary Plains Villagers in the area lived in rectangular houses (see **Huff Indian Village**).

Recovered artifacts include pottery, arrowheads, scrapers, flakes, grinding tools, bison shoulder-blade hoe fragment, butchered animal bones, and corn kernels and cobs. A pit filled with ash and a hearth were also uncovered. Charcoal from the hearth was radiocarbon dated to A.D. 1300 to 1400. Based on the archeological excavations, inhabitants occupying the site more than six centuries ago were involved in such activities as food preparation, hide processing, and stone-tool production and repair.

There are two markers at the site, one identifying it as a state historic site and the other placed there by the Order of the Masons.

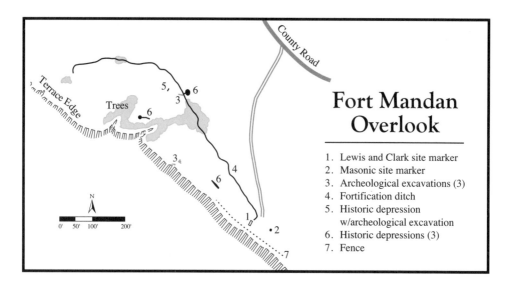

Fort Mandan Overlook

1. Lewis and Clark site marker
2. Masonic site marker
3. Archeological excavations (3)
4. Fortification ditch
5. Historic depression
   w/archeological excavation
6. Historic depressions (3)
7. Fence

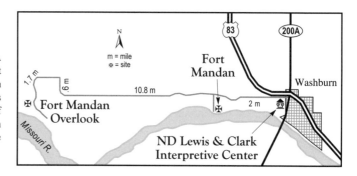

From: Junction US•83 and ND•200A at Washburn, McLean County (I-11):

☞ South .1 mile on ND•200A toward the Missouri River ☞ West 10.8 miles on gravel road ☞ North .6 mile ☞ West and south 1.7 miles to site access road on west side of road ☞ The site is marked by an aluminum plaque on a fieldstone marker.

For a list of state and national historic sites, museums, and parks nearby, see page 159.

✦ Fort Totten State Historic Site

Fort Totten is one of the best-preserved frontier military posts in the United States. Sixteen of the original military structures still stand at the Fort Totten State Historic Site, located in the town of Fort Totten in Benson County. The fort was built between 1867 and 1873 as a military outpost, but for most of its history it served as a boarding school for Indian children. The original garrison policed the surrounding military reservation, guarded overland mail and transportation routes, and provided both protection and oversight for the Dakota (Sioux) Indians living on the Spirit Lake Nation Reservation (formerly known as the Devils Lake Sioux Indian Reservation). Military units stationed at the fort always included infantry soldiers, and various detachments of the Seventh U.S. Cavalry were stationed at the post during the 1870s.

Decommissioned as a military post in December 1890, the buildings were transferred to the U.S. Department of the Interior for use as an industrial boarding school for Indian children. The first students, aged from five to twenty-one years, were primarily from the surrounding Dakota reservation. They were later joined by Chippewa children from the Turtle Mountain Indian Reservation and others, until at one time the boarding school had the largest student body (more than 400) of any of the schools in the federal system. Students received vocational and academic training in such skills as seamstress/tailoring, harness and shoe making, baking, farming, dairying, printing, and carpentry.

The industrial boarding school closed in 1935 when Fort Totten became the site of a tuberculosis preventorium, a five-year experimental program that placed children considered at high risk for contracting tuberculosis in a closed, controlled environment that provided both care and education. At the end of the program in 1940, Fort Totten again became a combination day-school and boarding school, with increased involvement by the local Indian community in its operation. A new school was opened in 1959, and the historic site was abandoned. In 1960 the site was designated as a state historic site.

121

Fort Totten (above, SHSND A1525), ca. 1898, during its use as an Indian boarding school. A teacher (right) supervises male Indian students in a tailoring class. This image was included in the school's catalog in 1913. SHSND 970.637 T641

The original brick military structures standing around the original parade ground are the adjutant's office, two first lieutenant's quarters, two second lieutenant's quarters, commanding officer's quarters, chaplain's and surgeon's quarters, hospital/chapel, commissary storehouse, quartermaster's storehouse, powder magazine, three company barracks, and bakery. An ADA-accessible boardwalk guides visitors to Fort Totten on a tour of these buildings, beginning with an introductory exhibit in the Fort Totten Interpretive Center in the restored commissary storehouse (Building 23). The exhibit describes the military, Indian school, and historic preservation activities at Fort Totten. While strolling around the parade ground one can explore several structures open to the public or view window exhibit panels describing the functions of key buildings. Buildings painted gray with red trim display the original military color scheme. Buildings painted white with green trim show the post-1904 Indian school color scheme.

The company barracks/main school (Building 14) is the home of the present-day Fort Totten Little Theater, where a local musical theater group stages productions during July. An Indian school classroom display as well as artifacts from Plummer's Mercantile Store of Minnewaukan, North Dakota, are exhibited in this building, and vending machine concessions are available. The site supervisor's administrative office is here also.

A gymnasium (Building 13) replaced what was originally a fourth company barracks building. At the time of construction in 1925 it was noted as the largest school gymnasium in the state.

The company barracks/boys' dormitory (Building 12) currently houses memorabilia from the North Dakota Odd Fellows/Rebekah Lodges. The first Odd Fellows lodge in what is now North Dakota was established in 1878 at the Fort Totten military post. Window exhibits also show the uses of the building as a military company barracks and as a boys' dormitory. The adjoining company barracks/boys' dormitory (Building 11) hosts traveling exhibits and features an audiovisual program about the history of Fort Totten.

An interpretive window exhibit is featured at the quartermaster's storehouse/bakery, laundry, and harness shop (Building 10). The powder magazine/school flour storage (Building 9) contains a display on the military use of the building. The hospital/school cafeteria (Building 7) is used by the Lake Region Pioneer Daughters as a museum. Another window exhibit is located in the second lieutenant's quarters/principal's office and print shop (Building 5).

The larger officers' quarters/school employee residence (Building 4) has been restored to an adaptive use as the Totten Trail Historic Inn through a cooperative agreement with the Friends of Fort Totten Historic Site. Overnight stays are available seasonally in rooms furnished in period styles from 1870 to 1910. Facilities are also available for meetings and receptions throughout the year. For information, call (701) 766-4874 or go to the web site, www.tottentrailinn.com.

The commanding officer's quarters, later the superintendent's quarters (Building 3), is partially restored and contains exhibits of life on "Officer's Row." Another officers' quarters/girls' dormitory (Building 2) has been partially restored and work is underway to install an interior walkway so visitors may view the building as a "demonstration unit" on historic preservation efforts at the site.

Fort Totten State Historic Site is listed on the National Register of Historic Places and is open year-round as an outdoor museum. Buildings are open to the public daily from May 16 through September 15. A fee is charged for admission to the site. State Historical Society of North Dakota Foundation members and children five and under are admitted free, school groups pay reduced admission.

Brochures describing Fort Totten are available at the site or from the State Historical Society of North Dakota. A book and videotape on Fort Totten history are also available for purchase. For more information, contact the Site Supervisor, Fort Totten State Historic Site, P.O. Box 224, Fort Totten, North Dakota 58335, call (701) 766-4441, or visit the web site at DiscoverND.com/hist.

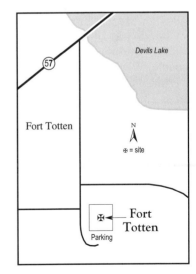

At: Fort Totten, Benson County (F-17):
☞ The site is located east of the road on the southeast edge of the town of Fort Totten.

For a list of state and national historic sites, museums, and parks nearby, see page 159.

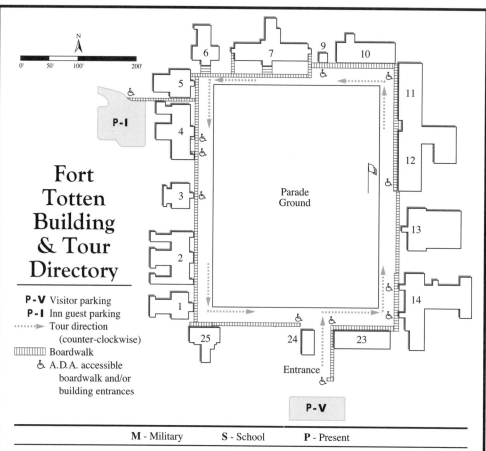

Fort Totten Building & Tour Directory

P-V Visitor parking
P-I Inn guest parking
········> Tour direction
         (counter-clockwise)
▨▨▨ Boardwalk
& A.D.A. accessible
   boardwalk and/or
   building entrances

P-I
P-V

N
0' 50' 100' 200'

6 7 9 10
5 11
4 12
3 Parade Ground
2 13
1 14
25 24 23
Entrance

M - Military	S - School	P - Present

1. 1871: **M**-2nd Lieutenant's Quarters; **S**-Girls' Sewing Room, Tailor Shop
2. 1871: **M**-Captain's and 1st Lieutenant's Quarters; **S**-Girls' Dormitory; **P**-Undergoing restoration
3. 1869: **M**-Commanding Officer's Quarters; **S**-Superintendent's Quarters; **P**-Undergoing restoration
4. 1869: **M**-Captain's and 1st Lieutenant's Quarters; **S**-Employees' Quarters; **P**-Restored to adaptive use as Fort Totten Historic Trail Inn
5. 1870: **M**-2nd Lieutenant's Quarters; **S**-Chief Clerk's Office, Principal's Office, Print Shop
6. 1870: **M**-Chaplain's and Surgeon's Quarters; **S**-Principal and Married Teachers' Quarters
7. 1870: **M**-Hospital and Chapel; **S**-Cafeteria; **P**-Pioneer Daughters' Museum
9. 1870: **M**-Magazine; **S**-Storage area
10. 1868: **M**-Quartermaster's Storehouse; **S**-Bakery, Harness Shop, Laundry
11. 1870: **M**-Company Quarters; **S**-Boys' Dormitory: **P**-Wildlife exhibit
12. 1869: **M**-Company Quarters; **S**-Boys' Dormitory: **P**-Odd Fellows and Rebekah Lodge memorabilia rooms
13. 1925: **S**-School Gymnasium
14. 1869: **M**-Company Quarters; **S**-Main school building; **P**-Site administrative office, Fort Totten Little Theatre, Pioneer Merchantile Store, Classroom exhibit, Concessions area
23. 1868: **M**-Commissary; **S**-Shop; **P**-Interpretive Center, Office, Restrooms, Gift shop
24. 1871: **M**-Bakery; **S**-Store; **P**-Shop
25. 1871: **M**-Adjutant's Office; **S**-School Offices

🏛 North Dakota Lewis and Clark Interpretive Center

Located at the intersection of U.S. Highway 83 and North Dakota Highway 200A at Washburn, the North Dakota Lewis and Clark Interpretive Center opened June 1, 1997. The center provides an overview of the Lewis and Clark Expedition, with special emphasis on the time the expedition spent at Fort Mandan during the winter of 1804-05. It features interactive exhibits, artifacts, and engaging displays that include a full-scale wood canoe carved from the trunk of a large cottonwood tree. Visitors can try on a buffalo robe and study a "cradle-board" much like the one Sakakawea may have used to carry her baby. The center also houses a gift shop and the Bergquist Gallery, which features rotating exhibits.

The new Fort Clark wing of the center tells the story of the Mandan and Arikara village and fur trade posts located at **Fort Clark Trading Post**, fifteen miles away off Highway 200A. Built as a fur trading post for the American Fur Company, Fort Clark became a cultural crossroads. Visitors to the site during the 1830s included Prince Maximilian of Wied and the Swiss artist, Karl Bodmer. The Interpretive Center contains one of only four galleries in the world to house a complete collection of Karl Bodmer prints. Bodmer's watercolors and Maximilian's written descriptions are considered among the most complete and reliable eyewitness accounts of the upper Midwest Indian cultures.

A pirogue, or canoe made from a hollowed-out cottonwood log (above, right), is one of the exhibit features of the North Dakota Lewis and Clark Interpretive Center.

While the focus of the interpretive center is the famous expedition of William Clark (left) and Meriwether Lewis (right, both SHSND A1827), the Fort Clark wing, completed in 2001, interprets fur trade history along the Missouri River.

The center is operated by the North Dakota Lewis and Clark Bicentennial Foundation in conjuction with the reconstructed **Fort Mandan** two miles north of the center. Both are open from 9 a.m to 7 p.m., Memorial Day through Labor Day. The remainder of the year the hours are from 9 a.m. to 5 p.m. There is an admission fee that covers both locations. Special rates are available for prescheduled school and group tours. For more information, contact the North Dakota Lewis and Clark Interpretive Center, P.O. Box 607, Washburn, ND 58577-0607, call (701) 462-8535 or toll-free (877) 462-8535, fax: (701) 462-3316, e-mail info@fortmandan.org, or visit the web site at www.fortmandan.com.

At: Washburn, McLean County (I-11):
☞ The center is located west of the intersection of US•83 and ND•200A.

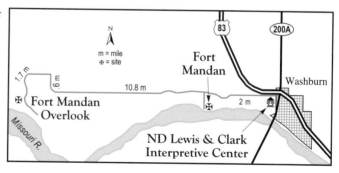

For a list of state and national historic sites, museums, and parks nearby, see page 159.

126

⬆ Palmer's Spring

Palmer's Spring State Historic Site, near Esmond, Benson County, marks the location where on August 23, 1868, six soldiers from the 31st Infantry and two civilian scouts escorting a mail wagon stopped for their midday rest and were attacked by Yankton and Blackfeet Indians. The Indians launched their attack from behind a large, limestone boulder (above, left), and three of the soldiers were killed in the first two volleys. Two other soldiers escaped to the safety of an earthen bank near the spring, and a civilian scout survived by hiding behind a wagon wheel. Fortunately, another civilian scout (Frank Palmer, above) and a soldier teamster had taken a horse to the spring for water and escaped the initial attack.

When Palmer and the teamster heard the commotion, they ran to the bluff above the spring where they fired at the Indians. The Indians were riding off on the soldiers' mules when two of the soldiers, the ones who had hidden in the spring bank, recovered their weapons and fired at them.

After the Indians withdrew, Palmer rode the one remaining horse to Fort Totten to get help. The surviving soldiers hid the mail and surplus arms and followed on foot. A relief party was dispatched from Fort Totten on August 24, 1868, and succeeded in recovering the wagon, mail, and supplies. The bodies of the dead were also taken back to Fort Totten for burial.

Palmer's Spring, the site of the battle, shows little change after the passage of more than a century. The limestone boulder surrounded by prairie grass stands at its original location (arrow, above). Frank Palmer (SHSND A3112), for whom the spring was named, spent the remainder of his life in the Fort Totten-Crary area and served as a delegate to the original North Dakota Constitutional Convention in 1889.

From: Esmond, Benson County (F-15):
☞ South 9.8 miles from the south edge of Esmond on asphalt/gravel road ☞ East 2.5 miles on gravel road ☞ The site is unmarked on the north side of the road.

For a list of state and national historic sites, museums, and parks nearby, see page 160.

⚒ Pulver Mounds

Pulver Mounds State Historic Site preserves two low, conical burial mounds (see arrows) on a small bluff above Coal Lake, southeast of Underwood, McLean County. Burial mounds such as these were typically constructed during the Woodland period from approximately 100 B.C. to A.D. 600 (see **Standing Rock**). At that time Woodland peoples buried their dead in a carefully prepared subterranean burial chamber, and then marked the cemetery with a round pile of earth over the grave, called a conical mound. Mound sites are complex cemeteries often used for hundreds of years; some are known to have been used for more than 1,000 years. Later, Plains Village groups sometimes used the tops of existing burial mounds as places of interment.

Conical mounds in North Dakota generally range in height from two to twenty-five feet, and in diameter from ten to sixty feet. The two mounds at the Pulver Mounds site are approximately forty-five feet in diameter and are three to five feet high. These burial grounds or cemeteries are sacred to many American Indians. In the state of North Dakota, mounds are classified as unmarked burial sites and are protected by law from disturbance.

To ensure preservation of Pulver Mounds, The Falkirk Mining Company donated this significant prehistoric burial site to the State of North Dakota with the State Historical Society acting as trustee. Access to the site is limited until nearby mining operations are completed. At present, there are no interpretive materials at the site. For access information, contact the Historic Preservation Division, State Historical Society of North Dakota, 612 East Boulevard Avenue, Bismarck, North Dakota, 58505, or call (701) 328-2666.

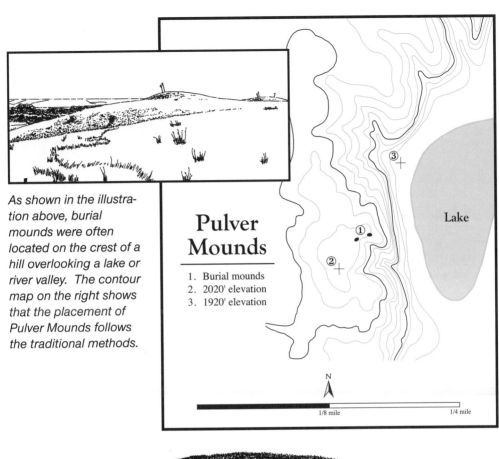

As shown in the illustration above, burial mounds were often located on the crest of a hill overlooking a lake or river valley. The contour map on the right shows that the placement of Pulver Mounds follows the traditional methods.

Pulver Mounds

1. Burial mounds
2. 2020' elevation
3. 1920' elevation

Lake

N

1/8 mile   1/4 mile

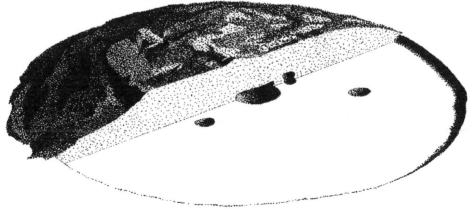

The cross-section, above, shows one stage of construction and related burial features in a burial mound. The dark circular depressions are graves.

✠ St. Claude

The St. Claude State Historic Site was deeded to the State of North Dakota in 1927 as a memorial to Father John Malo. It is located about two miles northwest of present-day St. John, Rolette County. The site contains the archeological remains of an 1882 mission and its cemetery. A stone marker on the site bears the inscription: "The Old Mission, St. Claude, May 3, 1882 by Pere J. F. Malo." A larger wooden sign describes some of the history of the site, and depressions mark several of the forty-seven graves recorded in the parish cemetery registry.

Father John Malo (inset, above, SHSND A6568), a missionary priest, came to the Turtle Mountains in 1881 with settlers from Quebec, Canada, to found a mission. He built a small log building, twenty feet by forty feet, with living quarters in the attic and a chapel on the main floor. Father Malo christened the mission St. Claude and opened the church on May 3, 1882. Later, the parish grew as Métis families moved in from the Red River settlements in Manitoba, and an addition, equal in size to the original building, was built onto the chapel.

When the St. Paul, Minneapolis, and Manitoba Railroad reached the area in the mid-1880s, it was decided that the church should be relocated closer to the railroad line. The St. Claude mission buildings were abandoned, and a new wood-frame church, St. John the Baptist, was built in 1887, two miles from St. Claude. This new church became the nucleus of the town of St. John.

From: St. John, Rolette County (B-15):
☞ North .25 mile on asphalt road ☞ West .25 miles on asphalt road ☞ North 1.25 miles on gravel road ☞ East .25 mile to end of dirt road ☞ The site is marked by a carved granite stone and a wooden sign.

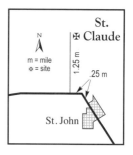

For a list of state and national historic sites, museums, and parks nearby, see page 160.

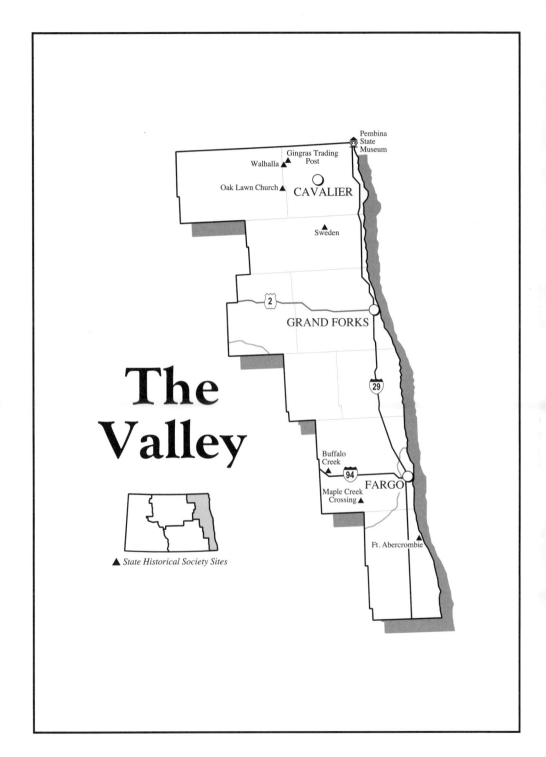

Pembina
State
Museum

Gingras Trading
Post

Walhalla ▲

Oak Lawn Church ▲ ○ CAVALIER

Sweden ▲

2

GRAND FORKS

29

The
Valley

Buffalo
Creek ▲

94

FARGO

Maple Creek
Crossing ▲

Ft. Abercrombie ▲

▲ *State Historical Society Sites*

⬧ Buffalo Creek

Buffalo Creek State Historic Site, in west-central Cass County, commemorates a point crossed by Sibley's expedition on August 15, 1863, on their way to Fort Abercrombie at the end of their summer campaign (see **Sibley and Sully Expeditions of 1863**). This was not, however, the full expeditionary force that had entered Dakota Territory on July 2, 1863. Colonel Samuel McPhail and his 1st Minnesota Mounted Rangers were scouting down the James River and would return to Minnesota by a different route.

After leaving Camp Arnold, Sibley's men marched nine miles southeast in the growing heat of a mid-August day. The expedition crossed the Maple River and continued another three and one-half miles to Camp Stevens, where they stayed the night. The expedition was about to leave Dakota Territory, after marching nearly one thousand miles, fighting three major battles and several skirmishes, and losing nine soldiers. It is estimated that they killed approximately three hundred Indians.

The modern Buffalo Creek State Historic Site is located about one-eighth mile east of the Maple River and about two miles northwest of the town of Buffalo. It is marked by a bronze plaque mounted on a boulder on the north edge of a gravel road. The plaque noting the expedition's crossing was installed in 1927 by the Dacotah Chapter of the Daughters of the American Revolution.

From: Buffalo, Cass County (K-20):
☞ West 2.25 miles on asphalt road ☞ The site is marked by a bronze plaque on a granite boulder north of the road.

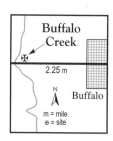

For a list of state and national historic sites, museums, and parks nearby, see page 160.

✦ Fort Abercrombie

Fort Abercrombie was established on August 28, 1858, on the Red River in Dakota Territory by Lieutenant Colonel John J. Abercrombie. Because of the threat of flooding in the bottomland area originally chosen for the fort, it was reestablished in 1860 at its present location on a high west bank of the Red River in what is now Richland County. After the post was abandoned in 1877, the town of Abercrombie formed one-half mile west of the historic fort location.

Known historically as "the Gateway to the Dakotas," Fort Abercrombie was the first permanent United States military fort established in what was to become North Dakota. It was also the only post in the area to be besieged by Dakota (Sioux) warriors for more than six weeks during the Dakota Conflict of 1862 (see **Sibley and Sully Expeditions of 1863**). During the Dakota Conflict, Minnesota Volunteer soldiers manned the fort when area settlers sought shelter there. The "regular" U.S. Army soldiers had been withdrawn during the Civil War and had been replaced by the Minnesota Volunteer Infantry. The fort was not protected by blockhouses or a palisade during the siege, but these defensive structures were constructed soon afterward.

The fort guarded the oxcart trails of the later fur trade era, military supply wagon trains, stagecoach routes, and steamboat traffic on the Red River (see maps on pages 95 and 137). It also was a supply base for two major gold-seeking expeditions across Dakota into Montana. Fort Abercrombie served as a hub for several major transportation routes through the northern plains.

After the fort was abandoned in 1877, fort buildings were sold and removed from the site. A Works Progress Administration (WPA) project in 1939-1940 reconstructed three blockhouses and the stockade and returned the original military guardhouse to the site. Beginning in the summer of 2001, a project to refurbish major portions of the WPA project and to reinterpret the site was initiated by the state historical society.

Fort Abercrombie State Historic Site is divided into two parts: a modern museum, park pavilion, and recreational facilities are located on the east edge of the town of Abercrombie; and the historic fort itself is located approximately one-fourth mile further

Ghosted buildings like the one in the foreground, above, at Fort Abercrombie help the visitor realize the layout of the original frontier fort.

Fort Abercrombie, Dakota Territory, 1863. SHSND A0363

east on Richland County Road 4, which bisects the historic site. From the parking lot on the north side of the county highway, visitors may walk around the interior square of the parade ground to view the reconstructed palisade, two reconstructed blockhouses, the original guardhouse, a reconstructed cannon bastion, several "ghosted" buildings, and informational markers describing the site.

Brochures describing Fort Abercrombie are available at the site or from the State Historical Society of North Dakota. Visitors may wish to begin their tour at the park museum, where additional information about the site is available.

Fort Abercrombie State Historic Site is open as an outdoor museum free of charge year-round. The museum is open Wednesdays through Sundays from May 16 through September 15. An admission fee is charged for the museum. State Historical Society of North Dakota Foundation members and children five and under are admitted free; school groups pay reduced admission. The park pavilion is available to groups on an advance rental agreement basis.

For more information during the summer season, contact the Site Supervisor, Fort Abercrombie State Historic Site, P.O. Box 148, Abercrombie, North Dakota 58001, or call (701) 553-8513. Information may also be obtained throughout the year by contacting the State Historical Society of North Dakota at (701) 328-2666 or going to the society's web site at DiscoverND.com/hist.

From: Abercrombie, Richland County (M-24):
☞ East on Broadway to east edge of Abercrombie ☞ The site museum is south of the road ☞ East of the museum the road bisects the fort reconstruction and parking space is north of the road and west of the stockade wall.

For a list of state and national historic sites, museums, and parks nearby, see page 160.

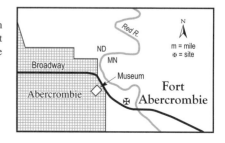

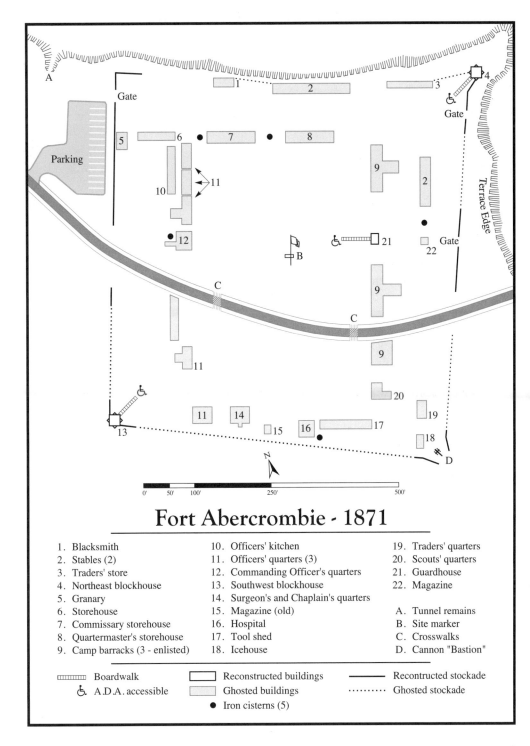

Fort Abercrombie - 1871

1. Blacksmith
2. Stables (2)
3. Traders' store
4. Northeast blockhouse
5. Granary
6. Storehouse
7. Commissary storehouse
8. Quartermaster's storehouse
9. Camp barracks (3 - enlisted)

10. Officers' kitchen
11. Officers' quarters (3)
12. Commanding Officer's quarters
13. Southwest blockhouse
14. Surgeon's and Chaplain's quarters
15. Magazine (old)
16. Hospital
17. Tool shed
18. Icehouse

19. Traders' quarters
20. Scouts' quarters
21. Guardhouse
22. Magazine

A. Tunnel remains
B. Site marker
C. Crosswalks
D. Cannon "Bastion"

▥▥▥ Boardwalk			☐ Reconstructed buildings	— Reconstructed stockade
♿ A.D.A. accessible			▨ Ghosted buildings	⋯⋯ Ghosted stockade
	● Iron cisterns (5)			

Antoine B. Gingras (left, SHSND 0200-4x5-282) as a young man and his home and trading post (background) today.

⌐ Gingras Trading Post

The Gingras Trading Post State Historic Site preserves the 1840s home and trading post of Métis legislator and businessman Antoine Blanc Gingras, northeast of Walhalla, Pembina County. Métis, meaning "mixed blood" or "mixed race," is a term used by people of combined Indian and European ancestry to describe themselves. Gingras was a prominent fur trader, who in 1861 claimed a net worth of $60,000 and later increased his holdings to include a chain of trading posts extending across northern Dakota Territory and southern Manitoba. Gingras's hand-hewn oak log store and home are among the few tangible remains of the fur trade in the Red River Valley.

Antoine B. Gingras was significant in the history of the region. In 1851 he was elected to serve in the Minnesota Territorial House of Representatives. He participated in the 1869 rebellion led by Louis Riel against the government of Manitoba to gain a national homeland and self-government for the Métis people. Gingras also took part in chartering the City of Winnipeg.

Both buildings on Gingras State Historic Site have been restored to their original appearance. While logs are exposed on the two-story trading post, clapboard siding covers the log structure of the house. The siding was added soon after the house was built. The house has been painted in its original historic colors, as determined by study of traces of the original paint. The exterior is deep red with white trim, and the interior reproduces the original color scheme of blue walls, yellow floors, pink ceilings, and green and brown trim. Interpretive panels and exhibits about Gingras, Métis heritage, and the fur trade are located in the restored house. Authentic reproductions of fur trade goods are sold in the Gingras store.

The site is listed on the National Register of Historic Places and is open from May 16 through September 15. Admission is free, and donations are accepted. For more information, contact the Site Supervisor, Gingras State Historic Site, R. R. 1, Box 55, Walhalla, North Dakota, 58202, or call (701) 549-2775.

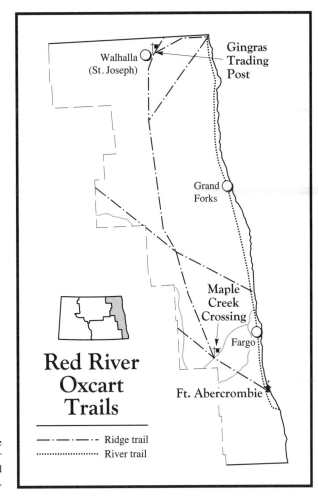

From: Walhalla, Pembina County (B-20):
☞ Northeast .5 mile on ND•32 to south edge of airport ☞ East .5 mile on gravel road ☞ Northeast .25 mile ☞ The site is marked by a sign and two buildings east of the road.

Red River Oxcart Trails

— · — · — · — Ridge trail
· · · · · · · · · · · · River trail

For a list of state and national historic sites, museums, and parks nearby, see page 161.

137

⊩ Maple Creek Crossing

Maple Creek Crossing State Historic Site recognizes a stream crossing important to travel in the days before bridges. With its gently sloping banks and firm bottom, this ford across the Maple River was a landmark in the early days of the exploration and settlement of Dakota Territory. Located three miles south of Chaffee, Cass County, the .38 acre historic site lies immediately east of St. Peter's Lutheran Church on a grassy terrace near a bend in the river. The actual stream crossing is approximately one-half mile northwest of the site marker.

Euro-American use of the crossing may have occurred as early as 1822, when discouraged members of the Selkirk Colonies moved from the Pembina area to the Mississippi River near Fort Snelling (St. Paul, Minnesota). They followed an early fur trade trail along the western edge of the ancient Lake Agassiz shore line that crossed the Maple River.

By 1843 oxcart brigades of Norman Kittson and "Jolly" Joe Rolette were fording the Maple River on an established trade route between St. Paul and the Canadian border settlements of Pembina and St. Joseph (see **Walhalla**). Six years later, Major Samuel Woods led a military reconnaissance expedition across the ford on a mission to "show the flag" to Métis settlers and recalcitrant Indians in the Pembina area, while gathering information about the region.

In 1851 Alexander Ramsey, governor of Minnesota Territory, used the crossing on a journey to Pembina. He was negotiating a treaty for the United States to buy five million acres of Chippewa land. The sale would have opened the Red River Valley area to Euro-American settlement. Although the Chippewa agreed, the United States Senate refused to ratify the treaty.

General Isaac I. Stevens, recently appointed governor of the newly created Washington Territory, crossed the river in 1853 while headed to the Pacific Northwest to assume his new duties. The journey also incorporated military exploration of the region to find a practical route for a transcontinental railroad. Nine years later, Captain James L. Fisk led a party of immigrants across the ford en route to newly discovered gold fields in Montana.

In 1863 the Sibley expedition returned to Minnesota via the ford (see **Sibley and Sully Expeditions of 1863**). Camp Ambler, the Sibley army's bivouac on August 17, 1863, was located southeast of the Maple Creek marker. By the time the troops reached the stream, they were nearly exhausted. The expedition's surgeons reported that 433 men were affected by the summer heat. Of these, 150 were so sick they had to be transported by ambulance for at least part of the day's march. The men rested and recuperated at Camp Ambler until leaving early in the morning of August 19.

A sod structure, located a half mile to the southeast, served as a shelter for mail carriers, freighters, and others traveling the Fort Abercrombie-Fort Ransom-Fort Totten trails during the 1860s and 1870s. A wood-frame store and inn replaced the sod building, operated from 1879 until 1883 by James N. Watson.

The modern-day Maple Creek Crossing State Historic Site displays a marker on a masonry base made of stone from the first North Dakota Capitol, which burned on December 28, 1930. Although no visitor services are available and the ford is not visible from the site, the state property is attractive, well tended, and accessible year-round.

From: Chaffee, Cass County (L-22):
☞ South 3 miles on gravel road ☞ East .6 mile ☞ South .25 mile on the west side of the Maple River ☞ The site is across from a church and is marked by an aluminum plaque on a fieldstone marker east of the road.

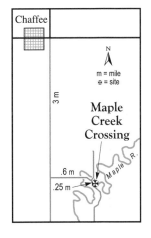

For a list of state and national historic sites, museums, and parks nearby, see page 161.

139

A fieldstone marker stands on the site of the Oak Lawn Church (left, SHSND A4440), which was destroyed by fire in 1954.

✠ Oak Lawn Church

At the junction of Highway 5 and Highway 32 in Pembina County, a peaceful cemetery rests in a grove of trees. Beside it, a fieldstone marker describes the log Presbyterian church that once stood near the cemetery, the Oak Lawn Church State Historic Site.

The Reverend Ransom Waite, Presbyterian minister from Mankato, Minnesota, settled in Beaulieu Township in 1883 to serve the surrounding communities. Two years later, the local congregation built a log church. Although the building lacked a floor when the first services were held, Waite and the trustees were soon able to secure a $300 loan from the Home Missions Board to install a permanent roof and floor. Planks served as seats until chairs and a pulpit were purchased a short time later.

To expand the use of the church, the congregation passed a resolution to allow any Protestant denomination to worship in the building, and as a result, Baptists and Methodists also held services there. Sometime prior to 1910, services were discontinued, but the local community continued to maintain the building and cemetery. The property was deeded to the State Historical Society of North Dakota on November 18, 1933. A grass fire destroyed the church on November 6, 1954.

From: Concrete, Pembina County (C-20):
☞ North 1 mile on asphalt road to junction of ND•5 and ND•32 ☞ The site is marked by an aluminum plaque on a fieldstone marker west of the road.

For a list of state and national historic sites, museums, and parks nearby, see page 161.

N
m = mile
✠ = site

32

5

Oak Lawn
Church

1 m E

Concrete

☗ Pembina State Museum

Situated at the border of Minnesota, North Dakota, and Manitoba, the Pembina State Museum, located off Exit 215 on I-29 in Pembina, tells the story of a region that has been a center of activity for centuries. The Pembina area was home to several groups of native peoples, including the Ojibwa, Dakota (Sioux), Assiniboin, and Cree. With their families, they lived, hunted buffalo, and gathered wild berries.

The region also played an important role in the fur trade business. From this trade a new nation of people were born, the Métis, who were descendants of European traders and Indian women. Early fur trade posts and colonies led to the establishment of a river town named Pembina. The scene of international politics and major transportation routes, the region has served as a gateway of commerce between Canada and the United States since the early 1800s.

The museum features a permanent exhibit gallery that presents 100 million years of the region's history, starting with fossils from a Cretaceous sea, to glacial Lake Agassiz, and extending to the present day. Visitors can learn about the diverse peoples who call Pembina home, including native Indian peoples and Euro-American settlers. Exhibits include stone and bone tools of the first peoples, a Red River oxcart, and other objects related to Pembina's fur trade industry. Other exhibits continue the story of the frontier military forts and the U.S. and Canadian border survey. The visitor can also explore the story of Euro-American agricultural settlement, including objects from Ukrainian and Icelandic settlers, and the transportation networks that continue to play a role in the economics of the region. A temporary gallery features unique exhibits from contemporary art to artifact-rich history.

The observation tower of the museum offers a stunning view of the Red River Valley from seven stories above the ground. On a clear day visitors have a 360-degree view for ten miles: a neatly organized patchwork of modern farmlands and evidence of the region's historic sites, industry, transportation, and communications. A travel information center contains information about other sites of interest in North Dakota. The museum store offers a unique selection of books and items, many crafted by North Dakotans, that reflect and enhance the museum exhibit themes.

The Pembina State Museum is open year-round. From May 16 to September 15, the hours are 9 a.m. to 6 p.m., Monday through Saturday and from 1 to 6 p.m. on Sunday.

From September 16 to May 15 the museum closes at 5 p.m. every day. The museum is ADA-accessible.

Admission is free for the exhibits and store but there is an admission fee for the observation tower. School and commercial bus tour group rates are available. For more information, contact the Pembina State Museum, P.O. Box 456, Pembina ND 58271 or (701) 825-6840 or mgrafe@state.nd.us. For information about the northeastern corner of North Dakota, call the Rendezvous Region Convention and Visitors Bureau at (800) 471-2381.

A view of the permanent exhibit gallery at the Pembina State Museum.

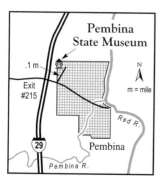

At: Pembina, Pembina County (A-22):
☞ North .1 mile from the east off-ramp of Exit #215 on I-29.

For a list of state and national historic sites, museums, and parks nearby, see page 161.

✠ Sweden

Established April 28, 1879, the Sweden post office and general store in present-day Walsh County was housed in a log building built by John Magnus Almen, who was the original postmaster. Later that same year, the post office moved to another log building on land owned by William McKenzie, and in January 1880, McKenzie officially replaced Almen as postmaster. The McKenzie enterprise soon expanded to include a livery barn, blacksmith shop, and a new frame house in this growing rural community. In September 1881, the position of postmaster changed hands again when Charles T. Wright was appointed to that position. The Sweden and Grafton post offices were authorized through the efforts of Thomas E. Cooper, who became Grafton's postmaster.

Mail delivery in the late 1800s was a challenging task. Mail was brought to Kelly's Point on the Red River by steamboat from Grand Forks. From there it was carried on horseback by Murdock McKenzie to Grafton and Sweden, a distance of twenty miles. When the Great Northern Railroad extended north from Grafton in 1882, the Sweden post office was discontinued.

All that remains of Sweden is a historical marker erected 450 yards north of its original location, which has been cultivated for many years. The marker can be seen just off North Dakota Highway 9, one and one-fourth miles west of Nash, Walsh County.

From: Nash, Walsh County (D-21):
☞ West 1.5 mile on asphalt road ☞ The site is marked by an aluminum plaque on a fieldstone marker south of the road.

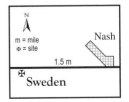

For a list of state and national historic sites, museums, and parks nearby,
see page 161.

✠ Walhalla

In 1842 Henry H. Sibley, American Fur Company trader, sent Norman W. Kittson to Pembina to replace Joseph Rolette Jr. as the head trader in the Red River Valley and International Boundary region. Kittson arrived in 1843 and established three new posts, including one in the vicinity of present-day Walhalla. This post may have been supervised by Antoine B. Gingras (see **Gingras Trading Post**). At about this same time, Rolette helped organize Red River oxcarts into a caravan to haul furs and hides to St. Paul.

The commercial activity generated by the oxcart trade drew many Métis families to the area, and by 1849 there was a resident population of one thousand. In 1852 Kittson moved to the growing community and built a store and warehouse. He was followed by Father George A. Belcourt, who built a chapel dedicated to St. Joseph. The community was subsequently named St. Joseph.

In March 1869 the Hudson's Bay Company surrendered possession of vast acres of land in Manitoba and Saskatchewan to the Dominion of Canada, which effectively eliminated the Métis quest for an independent homeland (the Riel Rebellion). This, along with the opening of a United States land office in December 1870 and the steep decline in the buffalo trade, assured the influx of European immigrants to the St. Joseph area. By 1877 only a handful of Métis lived in St. Joseph and quickly were replaced by Scandinavian immigrants. The town's name was soon changed from St. Joseph to Walhalla at the suggestion of James Wickes Taylor, U.S. Consul and settlement promoter.

In 1899 the Kittson store and warehouse were reportedly serving as stables for the

Bellevue Hotel in downtown Walhalla. In hopes of preserving a relic of the fur trade, one of the buildings was dismantled, moved, and rebuilt on its current location at Walhalla State Historic Site in 1904.

Today the log building sits on the edge of the Pembina Escarpment (Hair Hills) overlooking the town of Walhalla. A depression near the southeast edge of the park is reported to be a cellar from one of Alexander Henry's Hair Hills fur trade posts. In 1994 archeological test excavations at the site discovered American Indian pottery dating from 800 to 1700 and Euro-American artifacts dating from the early 1700s to the middle 1800s. A gravel parking lot, restrooms, interpretive sign, and a picnic shelter provide amenities for the visitor.

Norman Kittson founded the American Fur Company post at Pembina in 1843. SHSND A3161

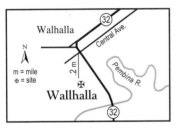

At: Walhalla, Pembina County (B-20):

☞ Southwest .2 mile on unmarked road from the intersection of ND•32 and Central Ave. in Walhalla ☞ The site is marked by an aluminum plaque on a granite boulder and a cabin at the end of the road.

For a list of state and national historic sites, museums, and parks nearby, see page 161.

Endnotes

1.   Elliott Coues, ed., *History of the Expedition Under the Command of Lewis and Clark* (New York: F. P. Harper, 1893; reprint, New York: Dover Publications, 1964), 1:236.

2.   Edwin James, *Account of an Expedition from Pittsburgh to the Rocky Mountains: Performed in the Years 1819,1820. . . . Compiled from the notes of Major Long, Mr. T. Say, and other gentlemen of the party.* (Frequently cited as James's Account of S.H. Long's Expedition 1819-1820. Part II of James's Account of S.H. Long's Expedition 1819-1820, "reprinted from the London 1823 edition."), 15:57-58, Reuben Gold Thwaites, *Early Western Travels: 1748-1846 . . .* (Cleveland: Arthur H. Clark, 1905). In Thwaites' *Early Western Travels*, James's Account of S. H. Long's Expedition 1819-1820 is in volumes 14-17.

3.   Robert C. Hollow and Herbert T. Hoover, *The Last Years of Sitting Bull* (Bismarck: State Historical Society of North Dakota, 1984), 1.

4.   Alfred W. Bowers, *Hidatsa Social and Ceremonial Organization*, Smithsonian Institution, Bureau of American Ethnology Bulletin 194 (Washington: U. S. Government Printing Office, 1965), 337.

5.   Enoch M. Eastman diary, July 3, 1863, Camp Buel [sic]. Enoch M. Eastman Papers. MSS 20010, State Historical Society of North Dakota (SHSND). Eastman was a teamster and a member of Company E, Hatch's Battalion, Minnesota, Volunteer Cavalry, 1865.

6.   "Diary of Unknown Soldier, June 16-August 27, 1863," July 23, 1863. Sibley Expedition Collection. MSS 10386, SHSND.

7.   O[scar] G[arrett] Wall diary, July 23, 1863. MSS 20181, SHSND. Wall was a civilian on the Sibley Expedition with the 5th Regiment, Minnesota Volunteer Infantry.

8.   L. B. Smith diary, July 23, 1863. MSS 20839, SHSND. Smith was a surgeon with the 7th Regiment, Minnesota Volunteers.

9.   George C. Pettie diary, July 23, 1863. MSS 20559, SHSND. Pettie belonged to Company A, 10th Regiment, Minnesota Volunteer Infantry, Steele County, Minnesota.

10.   John Danielson, "The History of Company G of the 7th Minnesota Volunteers, War of the Rebellion, 1862-1865," July 23, 1863. MSS 20559, SHSND.

11.   Ibid.

12.   Pettie diary, July 22, 1863.

13.   Eastman diary, July 14, 1863.

14.   Smith diary, July 14, 1863.

15.   Danielson, August 3, 1863.

16.   Danielson, August 2, 1863.

17.   Gary E. Moulton, ed., *The Journals of the Lewis & Clark Expedition* (Lincoln and London: Univeristy of Nebraska Press, 1996), 10:62.

Individual Site Features

Legend

◉ Historical Marker	◎ No Development	🏛 Museum	*i* Interpretive Center
✝ Visitor Center	☞ Guided Tour	↘ Overlook	$ Museum Store
✪ National Register	✪ National Landmark	R Restrooms	⊼ Picnic Area
■ Historic Building	◪ Reconstructed Historic Building		

Sites not a part of the State Historical Society of North Dakota historic site network are noted in italics.

Big Mound Battlefield	◉
Bismarck-Deadwood Stage Trail	◉
Brenner Crossing	◎
Buffalo Creek	◉
Camp Arnold	◉
Camp Atchison	◉
Camp Buell	◉
Camp Corning	◉
Camp Grant	◉
Camp Hancock	◉ ■ 🏛 ✪
Camp Kimball	◉
Camp Sheardown	◉
Camp Weiser	◉
Camp Whitney	◉
Cannonball Stage Station	◉ R ⊼
Chaska (Camp Banks)	◉
Crowley Flint Quarry	◎
David Thompson	◉
De Mores Interpretive Center	◉ 🏛 *i* ✝ $ R
Chateau de Mores	■ 🏛 ☞ ✪
de Mores Memorial Park	◉
de Mores Packing Plant	✪ ⊼
Double Ditch Indian Village	◉ ✪

Elkhorn Ranch Buffer Zone	◎										
Former Governors' Mansion	◉	■	🏛	✪							
Fort Abercrombie	◉	■	🏛	↟	$	R	🌲	◩			
Fort Abraham Lincoln SP	◩	🏛	*i*	↟	☞	$	R	🌲			
Fort Buford	◉	■	🏛	*i*	↟	✪	$	R	🌲		
Fort Clark	◉	✪	R	🌲							
Fort Dilts	◉	✪									
Fort Mandan	◩	↟	R	🌲							
Fort Mandan Overlook	◉	↘									
Fort Ransom	◉										
Fort Rice	◉	R									
Fort Totten	◉	■	🏛	*i*	↟	☞	$	✪	R		
Fort Union Trading Post NHS	◩	*i*	↟	☞	$	✪	R	🌲			
Gingras Trading Post	◉	↟	✪	$	R	🌲					
Hudson Townsite	◉										
Huff Indian Village	◉	✪									
Killdeer Mountain Battlefield	◉										
Knife River Indian Villages NHS	◩	*i*	↟	☞	$	✪	R	🌲			
Lake Jessie	◉										
Lake Johnson	◉										
Maple Creek Crossing	◉										
McPhail's Butte Overlook	◉	↘									
Medicine Rock	◉	✪									
Menoken Indian Village	◉	✪	✪								
Molander Indian Village	◉										
North Dakota Heritage Center	🏛	$	R								
North Dakota Lewis and Clark Interpretive Center	🏛	$	R								
Oak Lawn Church	◉										
Palmer's Spring	◎										
Pembina State Museum	🏛	$	R	🌲							
Pulver Mounds	◎										
Sitting Bull Burial	◉										
St. Claude	◉										
Standing Rock	◉										
Steamboat Warehouse	◉										
Stutsman County Courthouse	■	✪									
Sully's Heart River Corral	◉										
Sweden	◉										
Theodore Roosevelt NP	■	*i*	↟	☞	$	R	🌲				
Turtle Effigy	◎										
Wadeson Cabin	◉	■									
Walhalla	◉	■	R	🌲							
Whitestone Hill Battlefield	◉	🏛	R	🌲							
Writing Rock	◉	R	🌲								

More Places to Visit!

The following is a list of state and federal historic sites, parks, and local history museums within a 50-mile radius of each state historic site. Occasionally, highly recommended sites within a 100-mile radius are included. Each site can easily be located using the markings listed from North Dakota's state highway map (i.e., K-15).

Legend

⬥ State Park   ✪ National Park, Preserve, or Historic Site

🏛 State Historical Society Museums   🏛 Local History Museum or Interpretive Center

The West ---

Bismarck-Deadwood Stage Trail — M-10

Camp Hancock	Cannonball Stage Station	Double Ditch Indian Village
Former Governors' Mansion	Fort Rice	Huff Indian Village
Menoken Indian Village	Molander Indian Village	Sitting Bull Burial
Steamboat Warehouse	Sully's Heart River Corral	🏛 ND Heritage Center

⬥ Fort Abraham Lincoln State Park
🏛 Weinhandl Museum, Shields   🏛 Custer Trail Museum, New Salem
🏛 ND State Railroad Museum, Mandan
🏛 Almont Heritage Park & Museum, Almont
🏛 Flasher Historical Society Exhibit, Flasher
🏛 Grant Co. Historical Society Museum, Carson
🏛 ND Lewis and Clark Interpretive Center, Washburn

Cannonball Stage Station — N-9

Fort Rice	Huff Indian Village	Sitting Bull Burial
Sully's Heart River Corral	Bismarck-Deadwood Stage Trail	⬥ Fort Abraham Lincoln State Park

🏛 Weinhandl Museum, Shields   🏛 Flasher Historical Society Exhibit, Flasher
🏛 Almont Heritage Park & Museum, Almont
🏛 Grant Co. Historical Society Museum, Carson
🏛 ND Lewis and Clark Interpretive Center, Washburn

De Mores — K-3

De Mores Chimney Park	De Mores Memorial Park	Fort Dilts
⬥ Sully's Creek State Park	✪ Theodore Roosevelt National Park - South Unit	

🏛 Joachim Regional Museum, Prairie Outpost Park, and Dinosaur Museum, Dickinson
🏛 Golden Valley Co. Museum, Beach
🏛 Billings Co. Courthouse Museum, Medora
🏛 Museum of the Badlands, Medora

Fort Abraham Lincoln State Park — L-11

Bismarck-Deadwood Stage Trail Camp Hancock   Double Ditch Indian Village
Fort Rice   Huff Indian Village   Menoken Indian Village
Molander Indian Village   Steamboat Warehouse   Sitting Bull Burial
🏛 ND Heritage Center   ▲ Cross Ranch State Park
⊕ Knife River Indian Villages National Historic Site
⌂ Ft. Mandan   ⌂ Custer Trail Museum, New Salem
⌂ ND State Railroad Museum, Mandan
⌂ Oliver Co. Historical Exhibit, Center
⌂ Flasher Historical Society Exhibit, Flasher
⌂ Almont Heritage Park & Museum, Almont
⌂ ND Lewis and Clark Interpretive Center, Washburn

Fort Buford — F-2

Writing Rock   ▲ Lewis & Clark State Park
⊕ Fort Union Trading Post National Historic Site
⊕ Theodore Roosevelt National Park - North Unit
⌂ Frontier Museum, Williston   ⌂ MonDak Heritage Center, Sidney, MT
⌂ Buffalo Trails Museum, Epping
⌂ Lewis & Clark Trail Museum, Alexander
⌂ McKenzie Co. Pioneer Museum, Watford City

Fort Clark — J-10

Camp Hancock   Double Ditch Indian Village   Former Governors' Mansion
Fort Mandan   Menoken Indian Village   Molander Indian Village
Steamboat Warehouse   ▲ Cross Ranch State Park   ▲ Fort Abraham Lincoln State Park
▲ Fort Stevenson State Park   ▲ Sakakawea State Park   🏛 ND Heritage Center
⌂ Ft. Mandan   ⊕ Knife River Indian Villages National Historic Site
⌂ Custer Trail Museum, New Salem
⌂ Almont Heritage Park & Museum, Almont
⌂ Mercer Co. Historical Society Museum, Beulah
⌂ ND State Railroad Museum, Mandan
⌂ Oliver Co. Historical Exhibit, Center
⌂ Heritage Park & Museums, Garrison
⌂ ND Lewis and Clark Interpretive Center, Washburn

Fort Dilts — N-2

De Mores Chateau   De Mores Chimney Park   De Mores Memorial Park
▲ Butte View State Park   ▲ Sully's Creek State Park
⊕ Theodore Roosevelt National Park - South Unit
⌂ Pioneer Trails Museum, Bowman

Fort Rice — M-12

Camp Hancock   Cannonball Stage Station   Double Ditch Indian Village
Former Governors' Mansion Huff Indian Village   Menoken Indian Village
Molander Indian Village   Sitting Bull Burial   Steamboat Warehouse
Bismarck-Deadwood Stage Trail ▲ Fort Abraham Lincoln State Park 🏛 ND Heritage Center
⌂ Weinhandl Museum, Shields   ⌂ ND State Railroad Museum, Mandan
⌂ Flasher Historical Society Exhibit, Flasher
⌂ ND Lewis and Clark Interpretive Center, Washburn

Fort Union Trading Post National Historic Site — F-2

Fort Buford   Writing Rock   ♠ Lewis & Clark State Park
✪ Theodore Roosevelt National Park - North Unit
🏛 Frontier Museum, Williston   🏛 MonDak Heritage Center, Sidney, MT
🏛 Buffalo Trails Museum, Epping
🏛 Lewis & Clark Trail Museum, Alexander
🏛 McKenzie Co. Pioneer Museum, Watford City

Huff Indian Village — L-12

Camp Hancock   Cannonball Stage Station   Double Ditch Indian Village
Former Governors' Mansion   Fort Rice   Menoken Indian Village
Molander Indian Village   Sitting Bull Burial   Steamboat Warehouse
Bismarck-Deadwood Stage Trail ♠ Cross Ranch State Park   ♠ Fort Abraham Lincoln State Park
🏛 ND Heritage Center   🏛 Weinhandl Museum, Shields   🏛 Ft. Mandan
🏛 Custer Trail Museum, New Salem
🏛 ND State Railroad Museum, Mandan
🏛 Flasher Historical Society Exhibit, Flasher
🏛 ND Lewis and Clark Interpretive Center, Washburn

Killdeer Battlefield — I-5

De Mores Chateau   De Mores Chimney Park   De Mores Memorial Park
♠ Little Missouri State Park   ♠ Sully's Creek State Park
✪ Theodore Roosevelt National Park - North Unit
✪ Theodore Roosevelt National Park - South Unit
🏛 Dunn Co. Museum, Dunn Center
🏛 Old Grassy Butte Post Office, Grassy Butte
🏛 McKenzie Co. Pioneer Museum, Watford City
🏛 Joachim Regional Museum, Prairie Outpost Park, and Dinosaur Museum, Dickinson
🏛 ND Lewis and Clark Interpretive Center, Washburn

Knife River Indian Villages National Historic Site — I-10

Camp Hancock   Double Ditch Indian Village   Former Governors' Mansion
Fort Mandan   Menoken Indian Village   Molander Indian Village
Steamboat Warehouse   ♠ Cross Ranch State Park   ♠ Fort Abraham Lincoln State Park
♠ Fort Stevenson State Park   ♠ Sakakawea State Park   🏛 ND Heritage Center
🏛 Ft. Mandan   🏛 Custer Trail Museum, New Salem
🏛 Almont Heritage Park & Museum, Almont
🏛 Mercer Co. Historical Society Museum, Beulah
🏛 ND State Railroad Museum, Mandan
🏛 Oliver Co. Historical Exhibit, Center
🏛 Heritage Park & Museums, Garrison
🏛 ND Lewis and Clark Interpretive Center, Washburn

Molander Indian Village — J-11

Camp Hancock   Double Ditch Indian Village   Former Governors' Mansion
Fort Clark   Fort Mandan   Fort Rice
Huff Indian Village   Menoken Indian Village   Steamboat Warehouse
Bismarck-Deadwood Stage Trail ♠ Cross Ranch State Park   ♠ Fort Abraham Lincoln State Park
♠ Fort Stevenson State Park   ♠ Sakakawea State Park   🏛 ND Heritage Center
🏛 Fort Mandan   ✪ Knife River Indian Villages National Historic Site

☖ Custer Trail Museum, New Salem
☖ Almont Heritage Park & Museum, Almont
☖ ND State Railroad Museum, Mandan
☖ Oliver Co. Historical Exhibit, Center
☖ Mercer Co. Historical Society Museum, Beulah
☖ ND Lewis and Clark Interpretive Center, Washburn

Sitting Bull Burial — O-12
Cannonball Stage Station   Bismarck-Deadwood Stage Trail   Fort Rice
Huff Indian Village   ⚑ Fort Abraham Lincoln State Park
☖ Weinhandl Museum, Shields   ☖ Flasher Historical Society Exhibit, Flasher
☖ ND Lewis and Clark Interpretive Center, Washburn

Sully's Heart River Corral — L-7
Cannonball Stage Station   Bismarck-Deadwood Stage Trail
☖ Custer Trail Museum, New Salem
☖ Hettinger Co. Museum, Regent
☖ Almont Heritage Park & Museum, Almont
☖ Grant Co. Historical Society Museum, Carson
☖ Hebron Historical & Art Society Museum, Hebron
☖ Joachim Regional Museum, Prairie Outpost Park, and Dinosaur Museum, Dickinson
☖ ND Lewis and Clark Interpretive Center, Washburn

Theodore Roosevelt National Park (South Unit) — K-3
Chateau de Mores   De Mores Chimney Park   De Mores Memorial Park
Fort Dilts   Elkhorn Ranch Buffer Zone   ⚑ Sully's Creek State Park
✪ Theodore Roosevelt National Park - North Unit
☖ Joachim Regional Museum, Prairie Outpost Park, and Dinosaur Museum, Dickinson
☖ Golden Valley Co. Museum, Beach
☖ Billings Co. Courthouse Museum, Medora
☖ Museum of the Badlands, Medora

Theodore Roosevelt National Park (North Unit) — H-4
Chateau de Mores   De Mores Chimney Park   De Mores Memorial Park
Killdeer Mountain Battlefield   Elkhorn Ranch Buffer Zone   ⚑ Sully's Creek State Park
⚑ Little Missouri State Park   ✪ Theodore Roosevelt National Park - South Unit
☖ Joachim Regional Museum, Prairie Outpost Park, and Dinosaur Museum, Dickinson
☖ Old Grassy Butte Post Office, Grassy Butte
☖ Billings Co. Courthouse Museum, Medora
☖ McKenzie Co. Pioneer Museum, Watford City
☖ Museum of the Badlands, Medora
☖ Three Tribes Museum, New Town
☖ Dunn Co. Museum, Dunn Center

Writing Rock — C-2
☖ Buffalo Trails Museum, Epping
☖ Pioneer Trails Museum, Hanks
☖ Divide Co. Museum, Crosby

Prairies and Coteaus ---------------------------

Big Mound Battlefield — K-15

Camp Grant
McPhail's Butte Overlook
♣ Beaver Lake State Park
🏛 Melzer Museum, Woodworth

Camp Kimball
Menoken Indian Village
🏛 Foster Co. Museum, Carrington
🏛 Logan Co. Museum, Napoleon

Camp Whitney
Stutsman County Courthouse

🏛 Fort Seward Interpretive Center / Frontier Fort / Frontier Village / Stutsman Co.
    Historical Museum, Jamestown
🏛 ND Lewis and Clark Interpretive Center, Washburn

Camp Arnold — K-21

Buffalo Creek
Camp Sheardown
Lake Jessie
Standing Rock
♣ Fort Ransom State Park
🏛 Steele Co. Museum, Hope

Camp Atchison
Camp Weiser
Lake Johnson
Stutsman County Courthouse
🏛 T. J.Walker Historical Museum, Fort Ransom
🏛 Foster Co. Museum, Carrington

Camp Corning
Fort Ransom
Maple Creek Crossing
Wadeson Cabin

🏛 Griggs Co. Historical Museum, Cooperstown
🏛 Barnes Co. Historical Museum, Valley City
🏛 Fort Seward Interpretive Center / Frontier Fort / Frontier Village / Stutsman Co.
    Historical Museum, Jamestown

Camp Atchison — H-19

Brenner Crossing
Camp Kimball
Lake Jessie
♣ Turtle River State Park

Camp Arnold
Camp Sheardown
Lake Johnson
♣ Graham's Island State Park

Camp Corning
Fort Totten
Stutsman County Courthouse
♣ Shelver's Grove State Park

✪ Sully's Hill National Game Preserve
🏛 Steele Co. Museum, Hope   🏛 Northwood Pioneer Museum, Northwood
🏛 Griggs Co. Historical Museum, Cooperstown
🏛 McHenry Railroad Loop & Depot Museum, McHenry
🏛 Tofthagen Library and Museum and Finnish-American Historical Society Exhibit, Lakota
🏛 Fort Seward Interpretive Center / Frontier Fort / Frontier Village / Stutsman Co.
    Historical Museum, Jamestown

Camp Buell — N-22

Buffalo Creek
Fort Ransom
Standing Rock
🏛 Sargent Co. Museum, Forman

Camp Weiser
Hudson
Wadeson Cabin

Fort Abercrombie
Maple Creek Crossing
♣ Fort Ransom State Park

🏛 Bagg Bonanza Farm, near Mooreton
🏛 Dickey Co. Historical Park, Oakes
🏛 T. J.Walker Historical Museum, Fort Ransom
🏛 Lidgerwood Community Museum, Lidgerwood

Camp Corning — J-20

Camp Arnold
Camp Weiser
Standing Rock

Camp Atchison
Lake Jessie
Stutsman County Courthouse

Camp Sheardown
Lake Johnson
Wadeson Cabin

153

🔥 Fort Ransom State Park   🏛 Steele Co. Museum, Hope
🏛 Northwood Pioneer Museum, Northwood
🏛 Barnes Co. Historical Museum, Valley City
🏛 Griggs Co. Historical Museum, Cooperstown
🏛 McHenry Railroad Loop & Depot Museum, McHenry
🏛 Fort Seward Interpretive Center / Frontier Fort / Frontier Village / Stutsman Co.
    Historical Museum, Jamestown

Camp Grant — J-16

Brenner Crossing	Big Mound Battlefield	Camp Kimball
Camp Whitney	McPhail's Butte Overlook	Stutsman County Courthouse

🏛 Melzer Museum, Woodworth   🏛 Eddy Co. Museum, New Rockford
🏛 Foster Co. Museum, Carrington
🏛 Wells Co. Historical Exhibit, Fessenden
🏛 Fort Seward Interpretive Center / Frontier Fort / Frontier Village / Stutsman Co.
    Historical Museum, Jamestown
🏛 ND Lewis and Clark Interpretive Center, Washburn

Camp Hancock — L-20

Bismarck-Deadwood Stage Trail	Double Ditch Indian Village	Former Governors' Mansion
Fort Clark	Fort Mandan	Fort Rice Huff Indian Village
Menoken Indian Village	Molander Indian Village	Steamboat Warehouse
🔥 Cross Ranch State Park	🔥 Fort Lincoln State Park	🏛 ND Heritage Center

🏛 Fort Mandan   ✪ Knife River Indian Villages National Historic Site
🏛 Custer Trail Museum, New Salem
🏛 ND State Railroad Museum, Mandan
🏛 Oliver Co. Historical Exhibit, Center
🏛 Flasher Historical Society Exhibit, Flasher
🏛 Almont Heritage Park & Museum, Almont
🏛 ND Lewis and Clark Interpretive Center, Washburn

Camp Kimball — I-16

Brenner Crossing	Big Mound Battlefield	Camp Atchison
Camp Grant	Camp Whitney	Fort Totten
Lake Jessie	McPhail's Butte Overlook	Palmer's Spring
Stutsman County Courthouse	🔥 Graham's Island State Park	🏛 Melzer Museum, Woodworth

🏛 Foster Co. Museum, Carrington
🏛 Wells Co. Historical Exhibit, Fessenden
🏛 McHenry Railroad Loop & Depot Museum, McHenry
🏛 Eddy Co. Museum, New Rockford
🏛 Fort Seward Interpretive Center / Frontier Fort / Frontier Village / Stutsman Co.
    Historical Museum, Jamestown

Camp Sheardown — K-20

Buffalo Creek	Camp Arnold	Camp Atchison
Camp Corning	Camp Weiser	Fort Ransom
Lake Jessie	Lake Johnson	Maple Creek Crossing
Standing Rock	Stutsman County Courthouse	Wadeson Cabin

🔥 Fort Ransom State Park   🏛 Steele Co. Museum, Hope
🏛 LaMoure Co. Museum, Grand Rapids
🏛 Barnes Co. Historical Museum, Valley City

🏛 T. J. Walker Historical Museum, Fort Ransom
🏛 Fort Seward Interpretive Center / Frontier Fort / Frontier Village / Stutsman Co.
   Historical Museum, Jamestown

Camp Weiser — L-21

Buffalo Creek	Camp Arnold	Camp Buell
Camp Corning	Camp Sheardown	Fort Ransom
Hudson Townsite	Maple Creek Crossing	Standing Rock
Stutsman County Courthouse	Wadeson Cabin	⚑ Fort Ransom State Park

🏛 Dickey Co. Historical Park, Oakes
🏛 LaMoure Co. Museum, Grand Rapids
🏛 Barnes Co. Historical Museum, Valley City
🏛 T. J. Walker Historical Museum, Fort Ransom
🏛 Fort Seward Interpretive Center / Frontier Fort / Frontier Village / Stutsman Co.
   Historical Museum, Jamestown

Camp Whitney — K-15

Camp Grant	Camp Kimball	Big Mound Battlefield
McPhail's Butte Overlook	Menoken Indian Village	Stutsman County Courthouse
⚑ Beaver Lake State Park	🏛 Logan Co. Museum, Napoleon	
🏛 Melzer Museum, Woodworth	🏛 Foster Co. Museum, Carrington	

🏛 Fort Seward Interpretive Center / Frontier Fort / Frontier Village / Stutsman Co.
   Historical Museum, Jamestown
🏛 ND Lewis and Clark Interpretive Center, Washburn

Double Ditch Indian Village — K-11

Bismarck-Deadwood Stage Trail	Camp Hancock	Former Governors' Mansion
Fort Clark	Fort Mandan	Fort Rice
Huff Indian Village	Menoken Indian Village	Molander Indian Village
Steamboat Warehouse	⚑ Cross Ranch State Park	⚑ Fort Abraham Lincoln State Park
⚑ Sakakawea State Park	✪ Knife River Indian Villages National Historic Site	

🏛 ND Heritage Center   🏛 Fort Mandan
🏛 Custer Trail Museum, New Salem
🏛 Almont Heritage Park & Museum, Almont
🏛 Flasher Historical Society Exhibit, Flasher
🏛 ND State Railroad Museum, Mandan
🏛 Oliver Co. Historical Exhibit, Center
🏛 ND Lewis and Clark Interpretive Center, Washburn

Former Governors' Mansion — L-20

Bismarck-Deadwood Stage Trail	Camp Hancock	Double Ditch Indian Village
Fort Clark	Fort Mandan	Fort Rice
Huff Indian Village	Menoken Indian Village	Molander Indian Village
Steamboat Warehouse	⚑ Cross Ranch State Park	⚑ Fort Abraham Lincoln State Park
🏛 ND Heritage Center	✪ Knife River Indian Villages National Historic Site	
🏛 Fort Mandan	🏛 Custer Trail Museum, New Salem	

🏛 ND State Railroad Museum, Mandan
🏛 Oliver Co. Historical Exhibit, Center
🏛 Flasher Historical Society Exhibit, Flasher
🏛 Almont Heritage Park & Museum, Almont
🏛 ND Lewis and Clark Interpretive Center, Washburn

Fort Ransom — M-2

Buffalo Creek
Camp Sheardown
Maple Creek Crossing
Wadeson Cabin

Camp Arnold
Camp Weiser
Standing Rock
♠ Fort Ransom State Park

Camp Buell
Hudson Townsite
Stutsman County Courthouse
♠ Sargent Co. Museum, Forman

♠ Dickey Co. Historical Park, Oakes
♠ LaMoure Co. Museum, Grand Rapids
♠ Barnes Co. Historical Museum, Valley City
♠ T. J. Walker Historical Museum, Fort Ransom

Hudson Townsite — O-20

Camp Buell
Standing Rock
♠ Fort Ransom State Park

Camp Weiser
Wadeson Cabin
♠ Sargent Co. Museum, Forman

Fort Ransom
Whitestone Hill Battlefield

♠ Shimmin Tveit Museum, Forbes
♠ Dickey Co. Historical Park, Oakes
♠ LaMoure Co. Museum, Grand Rapids
♠ Coleman & Depot Museums, Ellendale
♠ T. J. Walker Historical Museum, Fort Ransom

Lake Jessie — H-19

Brenner Crossing
Camp Corning
Fort Totten
♠ Shelver's Grove State Park
❂ Sully's Hill National Game Preserve

Camp Arnold
Camp Kimball
Lake Johnson
♠ Turtle River State Park

Camp Atchison
Camp Sheardown
Stutsman County Courthouse

♠ Steele Co. Museum, Hope   ♠ Northwood Pioneer Museum, Northwood
♠ McHenry Railroad Loop & Depot Museum, McHenry
♠ Griggs Co. Historical Museum, Cooperstown
♠ Niagara Community Historical Society Exhibit, Niagara
♠ Tofthagen Library and Museum and Finnish-American Historical Society Exhibit, Lakota
♠ Fort Seward Interpretive Center / Frontier Fort / Frontier Village / Stutsman Co.
    Historical Museum, Jamestown

Lake Johnson — I-20

Brenner Crossing
Camp Atchison
Lake Jessie
♠ Steele Co. Museum, Hope

Buffalo Creek
Camp Corning
Stutsman County Courthouse
♠ Northwood Pioneer Museum, Northwood

Camp Arnold
Camp Sheardown
Wadeson Cabin

♠ Hatton-Carl Ben Eielson Museum, Hatton
♠ Barnes Co. Historical Museum, Valley City
♠ Griggs Co. Historical Museum, Cooperstown
♠ McHenry Railroad Loop & Depot Museum, McHenry
♠ Fort Seward Interpretive Center / Frontier Fort / Frontier Village / Stutsman Co.
    Historical Museum, Jamestown

McPhail's Butte Overlook — K-15

Big Mound Battlefield
Camp Whitney
♠ Beaver Lake State Park

Camp Grant
Menoken Indian Village
♠ Melzer Museum, Woodworth

Camp Kimball
Stutsman County Courthouse
♠ Logan Co. Museum, Napoleon

156

🏛 Foster Co. Museum, Carrington
🏛 Fort Seward Interpretive Center / Frontier Fort / Frontier Village / Stutsman Co.
    Historical Museum, Jamestown
🏛 ND Lewis and Clark Interpretive Center, Washburn

Menoken Indian Village — K-12

Bismarck-Deadwood Stage Trail	Big Mound Battlefield	Camp Hancock
Camp Whitney	Double Ditch Indian Village	Former Governors' Mansion
Fort Clark	Fort Mandan	Fort Rice
Huff Indian Village	McPhail's Butte Overlook	Molander Indian Village
Steamboat Warehouse	⛰ Cross Ranch State Park	⛰ Fort Lincoln State Park
🏛 ND Heritage Center	🏛 ND State Railroad Museum, Mandan	

🏛 ND Lewis and Clark Interpretive Center, Washburn

North Dakota Heritage Center — L-20

Bismarck-Deadwood Stage Trail	Camp Hancock	Double Ditch Indian Village
Former Governors' Mansion	Fort Clark	Fort Mandan
Fort Rice	Huff Indian Village	Menoken Indian Village
Molander Indian Village	Steamboat Warehouse	⛰ Cross Ranch State Park
✪ Knife River Indian Villages National Historic Site		⛰ Fort Abraham Lincoln State Park

🏛 Fort Mandan   🏛 Custer Trail Museum, New Salem
🏛 ND State Railroad Museum, Mandan
🏛 Oliver Co. Historical Exhibit, Center
🏛 Flasher Historical Society Exhibit, Flasher
🏛 Almont Heritage Park & Museum, Almont
🏛 ND Lewis and Clark Interpretive Center, Washburn

Standing Rock — L-20

Buffalo Creek	Camp Arnold	Camp Buell
Camp Corning	Camp Sheardown	Camp Weiser
Fort Ransom	Hudson Townsite	Maple Creek Crossing
Stutsman County Courthouse	Wadeson Cabin	⛰ Fort Ransom State Park

🏛 Sargent Co. Museum, Forman   🏛 Dickey Co. Historical Park, Oakes
🏛 LaMoure Co. Museum, Grand Rapids
🏛 Barnes Co. Historical Museum, Valley City
🏛 T. J. Walker Historical Museum, Fort Ransom
🏛 Fort Seward Interpretive Center / Frontier Fort / Frontier Village / Stutsman Co.
    Historical Museum, Jamestown

Steamboat Warehouse — L-11

Bismarck-Deadwood Stage Trail	Camp Hancock	Double Ditch Indian Village
Former Governors' Mansion	Fort Clark	Fort Mandan
Fort Rice	Huff Indian Village	Menoken Indian Village
Molander Indian Village	⛰ Cross Ranch State Park	⛰ Fort Abraham Lincoln State Park
🏛 ND Heritage Center	✪ Knife River Indian Villages National Historic Site	

🏛 Fort Mandan   🏛 Custer Trail Museum, New Salem
🏛 ND State Railroad Museum, Mandan
🏛 Oliver Co. Historical Exhibit, Center
🏛 Flasher Historical Society Exhibit, Flasher
🏛 Almont Heritage Park & Museum, Almont
🏛 ND Lewis and Clark Interpretive Center, Washburn

Stutsman County Courthouse — K-18

Big Mound Battlefield
Camp Corning
Camp Sheardown
Fort Ransom
McPhail's Butte Overlook
⚑ Fort Ransom State Park
🏛 LaMoure Co. Museum, Grand Rapids
🏛 Barnes Co. Historical Museum, Valley City
🏛 Fort Seward Interpretive Center / Frontier Fort / Frontier Village / Stutsman Co.
　　Historical Museum, Jamestown

Camp Arnold
Camp Grant
Camp Weiser
Lake Jessie
Standing Rock
🏛 Melzer Museum, Woodworth

Camp Atchison
Camp Kimball
Camp Whitney
Lake Johnson
Wadeson Cabin

Wadeson Cabin — L-20

Buffalo Creek
Camp Corning
Fort Ransom
Maple Creek Crossing
⚑ Fort Ransom State Park
🏛 Barnes Co. Historical Museum, Valley City
🏛 T. J. Walker Historical Museum, Fort Ransom
🏛 Fort Seward Interpretive Center / Frontier Fort / Frontier Village / Stutsman Co.
　　Historical Museum, Jamestown

Camp Arnold
Camp Sheardown
Hudson Townsite
Standing Rock
🏛 Dickey Co. Historical Park, Oakes

Camp Buell
Camp Weiser
Lake Johnson
Stutsman County Courthouse

Whitestone Hill Battlefield — N-18

Hudson Townsite
🏛 McIntosh Co. Heritage Center, Ashley
🏛 Shimmin Tveit Museum, Forbes
🏛 Dickey Co. Historical Park, Oakes
🏛 LaMoure Co. Museum, Grand Rapids
🏛 Coleman & Depot Museums, Ellendale

⚑ Beaver Lake State Park

⚑ Doyle Memorial State Park

Lakes and Gardens --------------------------------

Brenner Crossing — G-17

Camp Atchison
Fort Totten
Palmer's Spring
◐ Sully's Hill National Game Preserve
🏛 Foster Co. Museum, Carrington
🏛 Wells Co. Historical Exhibit, Fessenden
🏛 Eddy Co. Museum, New Rockford
🏛 Little Hoop Community College, Fort Totten
🏛 Minnewaukan Museum, Minnewaukan
🏛 Belle Isle Indian Gallery & Museum, St. Michael
🏛 McHenry Railroad Loop & Depot Museum, McHenry
🏛 Pioneer Daughters Library & Lillian Wineman Collection, Devils Lake
🏛 Tofthagen Library and Museum and Finnish-American Historical Society Exhibit, Lakota

Camp Grant
Lake Jessie
⚑ Graham's Island State Park

Camp Kimball
Lake Johnson
⚑ Shelver's Grove State Park

158

David Thompson — F-12
- ⛩ Soo Depot Transportation Museum, Minot
- ⛩ Ward Co. Pioneer Village & Museum, Minot
- ⛩ McHenry Co. Historical Society Museum, Towner
- ⛩ Geographical Center Pioneer Village & Museum, Rugby
- ⛩ ND Lewis and Clark Interpretive Center, Washburn

Fort Mandan — 1-10

Camp Hancock   Double Ditch Indian Village   Former Governors' Mansion
Fort Clark   Molander Indian Village   Steamboat Warehouse
Fort Mandan Overlook   ⚑ Cross Ranch State Park   ⚑ Fort Abraham Lincoln State Park
⚑ Fort Stevenson State Park   ⚑ Indian Hills State Park   ⚑ Sakakawea State Park
🏛 ND Heritage Center   ✪ Knife River Indian Villages National Historic Site

- ⛩ Custer Trail Museum, New Salem
- ⛩ Heritage Park & Museums, Garrison
- ⛩ Mercer Co. Historical Society Museum, Beulah
- ⛩ ND State Railroad Museum, Mandan
- ⛩ Oliver Co. Historical Exhibit, Center
- ⛩ ND Lewis and Clark Interpretive Center, Washburn

Fort Mandan Overlook — 1-10

Camp Hancock   Double Ditch Indian Village   Former Governors' Mansion
Fort Clark   Molander Indian Village   Steamboat Warehouse
⚑ Cross Ranch State Park   ⚑ Indian Hills State Park   ⚑ Fort Abraham Lincoln State Park
⚑ Fort Stevenson State Park   ⚑ Sakakawea State Park   🏛 ND Heritage Center
⛩ Fort Mandan   ✪ Knife River Indian Villages National Historic Site

- ⛩ Custer Trail Museum, New Salem
- ⛩ Heritage Park & Museums, Garrison
- ⛩ Mercer Co. Historical Society Museum, Beulah
- ⛩ ND State Railroad Museum, Mandan
- ⛩ Oliver Co. Historical Exhibit, Center
- ⛩ ND Lewis and Clark Interpretive Center, Washburn

Fort Totten — F-17

Brenner Crossing   Camp Atchison   Camp Kimball
Lake Jessie   Palmer's Spring   ⚑ Graham's Island State Park
⚑ Indian Hills State Park   ⚑ Shelver's Grove State Park   ✪ Sully's Hill Nat'l Game Preserve

- ⛩ Foster Co. Museum, Carrington
- ⛩ Wells Co. Historical Exhibit, Fessenden
- ⛩ Eddy Co. Museum, New Rockford
- ⛩ Little Hoop Community College, Fort Totten
- ⛩ Minnewaukan Museum, Minnewaukan
- ⛩ Belle Isle Indian Gallery & Museum, St. Michael
- ⛩ McHenry Railroad Loop & Depot Museum, McHenry
- ⛩ Pioneer Daughters Library & Lillian Wineman Collection, Devils Lake
- ⛩ Tofthagen Library and Museum and Finnish-American Historical Society Exhibit, Lakota

North Dakota Lewis & Clark Interpretive Center— 1-10

Camp Hancock   Double Ditch Indian Village   Former Governors' Mansion
Fort Clark   Molander Indian Village   Steamboat Warehouse
Fort Mandan Overlook   Sitting Bull Burial   ⚑ Cross Ranch State Park
⚑ Fort Stevenson State Park   ⚑ Indian Hills State Park   ⚑ Sakakawea State Park

- ⚑ Fort Abraham Lincoln State Park
- ✪ Knife River Indian Villages National Historic Site
- 🏛 Custer Trail Museum, New Salem
- 🏛 Heritage Park & Museums, Garrison
- 🏛 Mercer Co. Historical Society Museum, Beulah
- 🏛 ND State Railroad Museum, Mandan
- 🏛 Oliver Co. Historical Exhibit, Center
- 🏛 ND Heritage Center
- 🏛 Fort Mandan

Palmer's Spring — G-15

Brenner Crossing   Camp Kimball   Fort Totten
⚑ Graham's Island State Park   ⚑ Shelver's Grove State Park
✪ Sully's Hill National Game Preserve
🏛 Eddy Co. Museum, New Rockford
🏛 Wells Co. Historical Exhibit, Fessenden
🏛 Minnewaukan Museum, Minnewaukan
🏛 Tofthagen Library and Museum, Lakota
🏛 Sheridan Co. Pioneer Exhibit, Goodrich
🏛 Little Hoop Community College, Fort Totten
🏛 Geographical Center Pioneer Village & Museum, Rugby
🏛 ND Lewis and Clark Interpretive Center, Washburn

St. Claude — B-15

⚑ Lake Metigoshe State Park   ✪ International Peace Garden, Dunseith
🏛 Rolette Co. Museum, St. John   🏛 Towner Co. Historical Museum, Egeland
🏛 Dale & Martha Hawk Museum, Wolford
🏛 Bottineau Co. Museum / Country School, Bottineau
🏛 Turtle Mountain Chippewa Heritage Center, Belcourt

The Valley

Buffalo Creek — K-21

Camp Arnold   Camp Buell   Camp Corning
Camp Sheardown   Camp Weiser   Fort Ransom
Lake Johnson   Maple Creek Crossing   Standing Rock
Wadeson Cabin   ⚑ Fort Ransom State Park   🏛 Steele Co. Museum, Hope
🏛 Bonanzaville USA, Fargo   🏛 T. J. Walker Historical Museum, Fort Ransom
🏛 Barnes Co. Historical Museum, Valley City
🏛 Heritage-Hjemkomst Interpretive Center, Moorhead, MN
🏛 Children's Museum at Yunker Farm / Roger Maris Museum /
   NDSU-Germans from Russia Heritage Collection, Fargo

Fort Abercrombie — M-24

Camp Buell   Maple Creek Crossing   🏛 Bonanzaville USA, Fargo
🏛 Bagg Bonanza Farm, near Mooreton
🏛 Lidgerwood Community Museum, Lidgerwood
🏛 Richland Co. Historical Museum, Wahpeton
🏛 Heritage-Hjemkomst Interpretive Center, Moorhead, MN
🏛 Children's Museum at Yunker Farm / Roger Maris Museum /
   NDSU-Germans from Russia Heritage Collection, Fargo

Gingras Trading Post — B-20

Oak Lawn
☖ Heritage Village, Grafton
🏛 Pembina State Museum, Pembina
☖ Pembina Co. Historical Museum, Cavalier
☖ Cavalier Co. Museum, Dresden

Sweden
⚐ Icelandic State Park & Pioneer Heritage Center, near Cavalier

Walhalla/Kittson

Maple Creek Crossing — L-22

Buffalo Creek
Camp Sheardown
Fort Ransom
⚐ Fort Ransom State Park
☖ T. J. Walker Historical Museum, Fort Ransom
☖ Bagg Bonanza Farm, near Mooreton
☖ Barnes Co. Historical Museum, Valley City
☖ Heritage-Hjemkomst Interpretive Center, Moorhead, MN
☖ Children's Museum at Yunker Farm / Roger Maris Museum /
    NDSU-Germans from Russia Heritage Collection, Fargo

Camp Arnold
Camp Weiser
Standing Rock
☖ Bonanzaville USA, Fargo

Camp Buell
Fort Abercrombie
Wadeson Cabin

Oak Lawn Church — C-20

Gingras
⚐ Icelandic State Park
🏛 Pembina State Museum, Pembina
☖ Pembina Co. Historical Museum, Cavalier
☖ Cavalier Co. Museum, Dresden
☖ Jugville Museum, north of Grafton
☖ Walsh Co. Museum, Minto

Sweden
☖ Alsen Museum, Alsen

Walhalla/Kittson
☖ Heritage Village, Grafton

Pembina State Museum— A-22

Oak Lawn
Gingras Trading Post
☖ Heritage Village, Grafton
☖ Cavalier Co. Museum, Dresden

Sweden
⚐ Icelandic State Park & Pioneer Heritage Center, near Cavalier
☖ Pembina Co. Historical Museum, Cavalier

Walhalla/Kittson

Sweden — D-21

Oak Lawn
⚐ Turtle River State Park
☖ Walsh Co. Museum, Minto
☖ Heritage Village, Grafton
☖ Pembina Co. Historical Museum, Cavalier
☖ Jugville Museum, north of Grafton
☖ Niagara Community Historical Society Exhibit, Niagara

Gingras
⚐ Icelandic State Park & Pioneer Heritage Center, near Cavalier
☖ Manvel Museum, Manvel
☖ Walsh Co. Museum, Minto

Walhalla/Kittson
☖ Alsen Museum, Alsen
🏛 Pembina State Museum, Pembina

Walhalla — B-20

Gingras
⚐ Icelandic State Park & Pioneer Heritage Center, near Cavalier
☖ Heritage Village, Grafton
🏛 Pembina State Museum, Pembina
☖ Pembina Co. Historical Museum, Cavalier

Oak Lawn
☖ Cavalier Co. Museum, Dresden

Sweden

Other Sites and Parks ╌╌╌╌╌╌╌╌╌╌╌╌╌╌╌╌╌╌╌╌╌╌

North Dakota State Parks

- Butte View State Park — *6 mi. east of Bowman*
- Cross Ranch State Park — *30 mi. north of Mandan*
- Doyle Memorial State Park — *8 mi. southeast of Wishek*
- Fort Ransom State Park — *1 mi. south of Fort Ransom*
- Fort Stevenson State Park — *3 mi. south of Garrison*
- Icelandic State Park & Pioneer Heritage Center — *5 mi. west of Cavalier*
- Lake Metigoshe State Park — *14 mi. northeast of Bottineau*
- Lewis & Clark State Park — *19 mi. southeast of Williston*
- Little Missouri State Park — *17 mi. north of Killdeer*
- Sakakawea State Park — *1 mi. north of Pick City*
- Shelver's Grove State Park — *3 mi. east of Devils Lake*
- Sully's Creek State Park — *2-3 mi. south of Medora*
- Turtle River State Park — *22 mi. west of Grand Forks*

Federal Parks & Sites

- International Peace Garden — *13 mi. north of Dunseith*
- Sully's Hill National Game Preserve — *2 mi. east of Fort Totten*

Index

Aboriginal Americans

Military Affairs

Parks

Trade and Technology

Exploration and Settlement

Museums

State Government

North Dakota Historic Sites

1. Big Mound Battlefield
2. Bismarck-Deadwood Stage Trail
3. Brenner Crossing
4. Buffalo Creek
5. Camp Arnold
6. Camp Atchison
7. Camp Buell
8. Camp Corning
9. Camp Grant
10. Camp Hancock
11. Camp Kimball
12. Camp Sheardown
13. Camp Weiser
14. Camp Whitney
15. Cannonball Stage Station
16. Chaska (Camp Banks)
17. Crowley Flint Quarry
18. David Thompson
19. De Mores
20. Double Ditch Indian Village
21. Elkhorn Ranch Buffer Zone
22. Former Governors' Mansion
23. Fort Abercrombie
24. Fort Abraham Lincoln S.P.
25. Fort Buford
26. Fort Clark Trading Post
27. Fort Dilts
28. Fort Mandan
29. Fort Mandan Overlook
30. Fort Ransom
31. Fort Rice
32. Fort Totten
33. Fort Union Trading Post N.H.S.
34. Gingras Trading Post
35. Hudson Townsite
36. Huff Indian Village
37. Killdeer Mountain Battlefield
38. Knife River Indian Villages N.H.S.
39. Lake Jessie
40. Lake Johnson
41. Maple Creek Crossing
42. McPhail's Butte Overlook
43. Medicine Rock
44. Menoken Indian Village
45. Molander Indian Village
46. North Dakota Heritage Center
47. North Dakota Lewis and Clark Interpretive Center
48. Oak Lawn Church
49. Palmer's Spring
50. Pembina State Museum
51. Pulver Mounds
52. Sitting Bull Burial
53. St. Claude
54. Standing Rock
55. Steamboat Warehouse
56. Stutsman County Courthouse
57. Sully's Heart River Corral
58. Sweden
59. Theodore Roosevelt N.P.
60. Turtle Effigy
61. Wadeson Cabin
62. Walhalla
63. Whitestone Hill Battlefield
64. Writing Rock

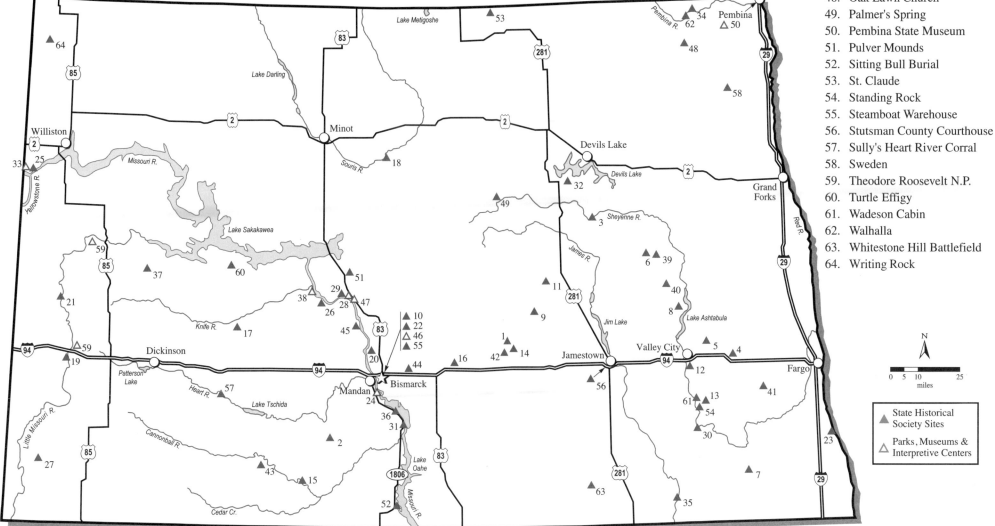

▲ State Historical Society Sites

△ Parks, Museums & Interpretive Centers